Appraising
Managers
as Managers

Appraising
Managers
as Managers

HAROLD KOONTZ

McGRAW-HILL BOOK COMPANY
New York   St. Louis   San Francisco   Düsseldorf   Johannesburg
Kuala Lumpur   London   Mexico   Montreal   New Delhi
Panama   Rio de Janeiro   Singapore   Sydney   Toronto

This book was set in Alphatype Astro by University Graphics, Inc., and printed on permanent paper and bound by Vail Ballou Press, Inc. The editors were Dale L. Dutton and Don A. Douglas. The designer was Naomi Auerbach. Teresa F. Leaden supervised production.

To Lyndall F. Urwick
Management pioneer, eminent consultant,
renowned scholar and valued friend.

Contents

4

Appendixes   187

Appendixes   187

Preface

One of the weakest links in management has been the evaluation of managers. Even though we have long been aware of the importance of managers for effective and efficient operation of business, government, and other enterprises, we have not had until very recently an accurate way of knowing whether practicing managers were really adequate for their jobs. Traditional appraisal of managers on the elusive standards of personal traits or work qualities has been both ineffective and illusory.

Throughout organizational history there has been an appreciation that groups of people work toward the achievement of objectives. But only lately have we come to realize that, to be meaningful, objectives must be actionable and verifiable and that the measure of managerial effectiveness should be a demonstrated ability to lead groups toward the attainment of such goals.

The current widespread interest in management by objectives owes much of its origin to a search for means of appraising managers. Disillusioned by the subjectivity of traits and work qualities, intelligent practitioners have understandably looked at what the purpose of organized activity is and the basic task of a manager in acting as a catalytic force in enterprise operation. It therefore became natural and logical to appraise managers against the standard of their most important criteria of performance—the setting and achievement of objectives.

That this has been a tremendous step forward, no one would deny. But experience has taught us several things. As simple as the concept of managing and appraising managers by objectives is, it still is a difficult approach to put into successful practice. Far too many enterprises have given lip service to the approach and too few have taken full advantage of its potential. Also, the system of appraising managers against setting and achieving objectives has been subject to the major deficiency that it does not allow for appraising managers as managers.

The purpose of this book is to set forth an appraisal program that emphasizes both appraisal against objectives and appraisal of managers as managers. As for the first aspect of appraisal we now have enough experience to appreciate exactly what is involved and to identify the strengths and weaknesses of the system and its practice. With regard to the second aspect of the program, the appraisal of managers as managers, an approach is suggested here to furnish at least a start toward giving this aspect of appraisal some practical meaning.

The conclusions and suggestions in this book are based upon participation in and experience with appraisal in both business and government operations, as well as research and experience reported by many practitioners and scholars. The system of appraisal of managers as managers was devised some years ago by the author. It arose from the belief that, if we are to appraise the quality of managing, the evaluation should be undertaken against the standards of management fundamentals.

In order to test the system, it was applied for five years in a medium sized multinational company. In this clinical application the program was given force by not only being an integral part of managerial appraisal but these appraisals were actually used in the upper middle and top management groups as one of two major criteria against which bonuses were allocated. Nevertheless, despite testing in the demanding environment of reality and being subject to the scrutiny of a number of practicing executives, the system of appraising managers as managers is offered as a still somewhat experimental answer to the problem.

In the development of this book the author owes a debt to the number of business and governmental organizations that have given him an opportunity to work with them on their programs as well as those graduate students who undertook research in the field under his supervision, and the many researchers who have reported their findings and offered their ideas in print. But he is especially grateful for the co-operation and criticism of Charles E. Hopping, Hugh S. Livie, Kenneth M. Bishop, and Vernis W. Clark, former members of top management and directors of Roberts Consolidated Industries, Inc., now a part of U.S. Plywood-Champion Papers, Inc. Helpful criticism was also offered by Harold F. Smiddy, formerly of the General Electric Company, Norb Krabuss of Hornblower & Weeks Hemphill Noyes, I. B. Jenkins of Radio Corporation of America, and Leonard A. Johnson of Four Star International, Inc.

The author is also indebted to Mrs. Helen Schwartz who so patiently and intelligently prepared the manuscript for publication.

It is a pleasure to acknowledge the valued assistance of those named above and the other sources of help for which footnote credit is given in the book. But, obviously, none of these can assume any responsibility for the deficiencies of the end product presented here.

Harold Koontz

chapter one

Managerial Appraisal: Key to Management

Managerial appraisal has sometimes been referred to as the Achilles heel of management development. But one could say more. It is probably the key to managing itself. It is important to management development, of course, because if a manager's strengths and weaknesses are not known, it would only be accidental that development efforts would be aimed in the right direction. Appraisal is, or should be, an integral part of managing itself. If a man cannot set objectives and the means of reaching them, planning and ability to achieve plans suffer. If he does a poor job of organizing and manning the organization structure, even the best plan will go awry because those who must contribute toward its attainment will either not know what their roles are or be unable to fill them. Much the same can be said for managerial directing, leading, and controlling.

1

In speaking of managerial appraisal, it should be clear that we speak of appraisal of the person in the job and not the evaluation of the position itself. Job evaluation is an important area of appraisal because status, compensation, and other perquisites should necessarily reflect the position. This area of evaluation, among managerial positions at least, is still largely one of subjective judgment and comparing one job with another both inside the enterprise and in other similar organizations. But it is not the concern of this book.

It is commonplace to say that the task of the manager is to set goals and methods of their attainment, and to enlist the support of people for whom he is responsible in working toward making plans happen. Therefore, if a company, a government agency, a charitable organization, or even a university is to reach its goals effectively and efficiently, ways of accurately measuring management performance must be found and implemented.

The Problem of Managerial Appraisal

There has long been a reluctance on the part of one manager to appraise another. In an activity as important as managing, there should be no reluctance in measuring managerial performance as effectively as we can, nor in having superior managers appraise the work of those who report to them. No one should get excited about the concern of those who fear that measuring the performance of others tends to put a manager in the untenable position of judging the personal worth of his subordinates and of acting on these judgments. It is sometimes difficult to comprehend this fear of "playing God" in a culture where individual performance has been rated at least from the time a person enters kindergarten and throughout his school and university life. In almost all forms of group enterprise, whether in work or play, performance has long been rated in some way. Moreover, most people, and particularly people of ability, *want to know* how well they are doing.

It is difficult to believe that the controversy, misgivings, even the disillusionment, still so widespread, with respect to managerial performance appraisal have come from the fact of measuring and evaluating. It rather appears that they have arisen from the things measured, the standards used, and the way measurement is done. A manager can understandably take exception, feel unhappy, or resist when he believes that he is evaluating, or is being evaluated, inaccurately or against standards that are inapplicable, inadequate, or subjective.

A bright beam of light and hope has emerged in the past decade and offers promise of making evaluation effective. The exploding interest in evaluating managers by comparing actual performance against preset verifiable objectives or goals is one of the most exciting developments in management in the past quarter century. However, examination of actual programs in operation raises questions as to how many of these programs are truly effective. Indeed, a fair question may be raised as to whether there is still more talk than action. In addition, one might question whether this outbreak of attention may become a fad and like other fads, even though based on sound principles, may fade from the scene. People have a way of becoming disenchanted and resistant when new ideas or programs do not work as intended.

Moreover, appraisal against verifiable objectives is not enough. As will be seen later in Chapters 5 and 6, this appraisal needs to be supplemented by appraisal of managers as managers. Moreover, neither system is without difficulties and pitfalls, and neither can be operated by simply adopting the technique and using the paper work. One must know and do more.

Before we can understand management appraisal and make

it effective, we need a clear understanding of the task of the manager, exactly why appraisal is so important a key, what we should be measuring, and what the requirements are for an effective appraisal system. Beyond this, the effective manager will be helped in knowing why traditional appraisal systems have failed in their purpose, what a workable program of appraisal against objectives is, and how we might supplement this by appraising managers as managers.

This is, thus, meant to be a "what-to-do" and a "how-to-do-it" book. It is based on clinical experience, research, and observation of the problem of appraisal in a variety of operations in a variety of cultures. While the book does not pretend to be the last word, it is hoped that the serious executive will be helped in his ability to use such research and experience as is represented here in solving the difficult problem of appraisal.

What Is the Task of the Manager?

It is too simple to say that the job of the manager is to get things done through other people. This time-honored concept even smacks of a degree of psychiatric manipulation of people. As every astute manager knows, no matter how much he may enjoy playing with people's minds and personalities, there is nothing more futile than trying to be an amateur psychiatrist. Even the professionals have far greater difficulty in doing this than they would like.

The task of the manager is one of selecting goals and designing and maintaining an environment that makes possible —even unavoidable—the performance of individuals working together in a group to attain these goals. Both in selecting goals and in creating an environment for performance, the manager must act in the light of the milieu in which he operates, including not only that of the enterprise of which he is a part but also the external environment—economic, technological, social, political, and ethical—in which his enterprise operates. To recognize and be responsive to these various environments is to be responsible *in the manager's own self-interest.*

Commonality of Understood Purpose While there are many elements of a suitable internal environment that the manager should create, there are a few which seem to outweigh all others. One element must be a commonality of understood purpose—objectives, clear and verifiable, and understood by all those in the group who are expected to contribute to their attainment. People must fill roles. Yet no meaningful role can exist without a goal, and no goal can be meaningful unless it is verifiable in the sense that people know what they are striving to attain and whether and when they have achieved it.

An Intentional Structure of Roles A second major element in this internal environment is the existence of an intentional structure of roles. In addition to a verifiable goal or objective, for a role to exist it must include a defined area of discretion (organization authority), a set of tasks or duties, and an understanding and availability of information sources throughout the organization. As can be seen, any given role may be narrow in task content and discretionary element, or it may be broad. In any case, these roles must be structured and, preferably, intentionally structured. There can be no team effort without a structure of roles. Even a pickup sandlot game soon develops structure. This is, of course, saying that formal organization must exist, but it can be readily seen that real formal organization implies much more than an organization chart.

An Environment Inducing Performance A third major environmental element is the existence of guidelines, techniques, or situations where people perform, preferably because they want to, often because this is the way things most easily get accomplished, and sometimes because things must be done in a certain way. Few roles indeed have no elements of conformity. For example, accounting, tax, and other systems require given action in the interests of control, safety, or efficiency. A bank would hardly want a teller using broad discretion in cashing checks, and an airline would certainly not want a highly imaginative, experimental, nonconformist pilot in the cockpit.

The Removal of Obstructions to Performance   A fourth feature of the environment to be created and maintained by a manager is one where every manager regards as a part of his job the removal of obstructions to performance of the persons for whom he is responsible. While some obstructions are beyond his control, he has not done his job until he has tried by every means at his disposal, including going "upstairs" with a suggested solution, to remove them. Admittedly, this is a simple concept, but too few managers in practice do what they can to recognize and remove these obstructions. Most managers would be surprised at the number of these obstacles, if their subordinates were encouraged to submit to them a list of things that were keeping them from performing effectively.

An Environment of Clarity   Finally, the environment must be one of clarity. Observations of management problems over many years disclose that a high percentage of difficulties are due to the fact that someone does not understand objectives, policies, procedures, programs, position descriptions, authority delegations, or many other ingredients of the managerial operation. Many managers try to be clear by weaving into a role or a system of roles a myriad of rules, procedures, and other detail that may clarify but do so at the expense of placing subordinates in unintended straitjackets. It is a difficult thing to be clear without being detailed.

Surplus Is the Goal of Every Manager

Both from the logic of his position and the social needs of group action, every manager in every kind of enterprise and at every level should have a "surplus" goal. He should so manage that his group attains an objective, whatever it may be, with the minimum of costs—in material and human resources, including in the latter, of course, such human resource attributes as time, effort, and dissatisfaction. Or, to put it another way, a manager's goal must be to gain as much of a purpose as possible with the resources at his command.

Profit Is Surplus   Business, being a type of activity designed to provide economic goods and services, expresses its enterprise surplus as profit. But profit is nothing more than a surplus of revenues over expenses. Government managers often say that they are at a disadvantage in comparison with business, that they have no profit by which to gauge their success. While it is true that government agencies, except those in a quasi-business operation, do not have a profit objective in the conventional sense of the term, it is nonetheless true that they should have a surplus goal. In other words, whatever the purpose entrusted by society to a government agency, it is reasonable to expect that the group charged with accomplishing this purpose and those who manage it should accomplish it with a minimum of resources, with as much "surplus" as possible. A chief of police, for example, has the duty to obtain as effective a police protection service as possible with the human and material means available to him.

Likewise, except for those managers who have charge of an integrated operation and who can be said to have real profit responsibility, managers of parts of businesses cannot have responsibility for profits in the normal use of the term. Nevertheless, each of their operations from marketing director to foreman of a machine shop should have clear objectives and the obligation to accomplish them in a "surplus" way.

Surplus Goal Requires Verifiable Objectives   If surplus is to have any practical significance for management, the objectives of any department or section of a company must be verifiable and also contribute toward the attainment of objectives of the total enterprise. There can be no measure of effectiveness without verifiable objectives, since no one can ascertain whether he is accomplishing a vague objective. There also can be no measure of efficiency of an operation without knowing output. Without verifiable objectives we may have input, but measuring efficiency requires knowledge of both input and output.

For far too many years and for still too many business firms, even now, it has been customary to say something like: "It is our objective to make a fair profit while making and selling a quality product, and being a good citizen in the community." Nice sounding, but virtually meaningless since no one can ever know whether these objectives are, in fact, being accomplished. Or we may say, as has often been said of a university, that "Our objective is to discover new knowledge and disseminate knowledge." Such objectives are hardly very meaningful and do not make possible the operation of a surplus objective by a manager or, for that matter, by a professor.

One of the exciting developments in recent years has been the attention given to development of verifiable objectives. A business may say, hopefully with some knowledge that attainment is possible with "stretch" or "pull," that "our objective is to make A dollars of profit in B product lines with C annual sales by D date"; or a manufacturing manager may say that his objective is to produce X number of Y products at Z cost.

Even in noneconomic enterprises, verifiable objectives are possible. But using them is rare in noneconomic enterprises even though, with proper analysis and thinking, they can be developed for any managerial or nonmanagerial position. It is exactly this, as will be seen in Chapter 3, that has resulted from effective programs of management by objectives.

Why Is Appraisal the Key to Management?

There are many persuasive reasons why appraisal is the key to management. There can be no argument as to the key role of managers themselves in assuring enterprise success. To be sure, money can be made by brilliance in marketing, engineering, manufacturing, or finance. A businessman can also be lucky by being in the right place at the right time, such as the West Coast machine shops at the beginning of World War II or the aircraft manufacturers of that time. However, few would doubt that, while nonmanagerial factors may account for initial success, in the long run the quality and vigor of management make the difference.

According to all available information, Henry Ford I was not a very able top manager, but his genius in perceiving and effectively pursuing concepts of mass marketing and mass production brought great wealth to himself and his company. It is likewise true that data, disclosed when the Ford Motor Company went public with its stock, told a story of heavy operating losses in the latter years of his leadership. Perhaps that company would have even gone bankrupt had not Henry Ford II turned it around by recruiting effective managers and putting in modern management techniques.

Without attempting to downgrade the importance of entrepreneurial genius and the profit-making potential of nonmanagement factors, no company can hope for long to enjoy prosperous growth without strong management. It is the purpose of effective managerial appraisal to assure just that.

In assuring effective management, it is axiomatic that managers must be developed, must be compensated in a way and to an extent to assure their proper motivation, and must know what is expected of them and how they are doing.

A common mistake in practice is to put a man in a program of development without knowing what his weaknesses and strengths are. Another common error is to base compensation and other inducements, as well as how well a man is doing, on purely subjective judgment. These mistakes may be unavoidable without a good system of evaluation. But these commonplace errors could be largely avoided with a program of effective evaluation.

Likewise, if a company or any other kind of enterprise is to assure that it will continually have strong management, selection and promotion of managers should be based on the most objective and accurate management appraisal possible. Even with the best possible appraisal, there is considerable risk in selecting and promoting. One can never tell for sure how good a man is until he is actually in a position. This usually takes time to know, and the higher the position, the more time. Mistakes mean more than a loss of costs in a man's salary and expenses. The time lost is ordinarily even more costly.

What Should Be Measured?

It hardly seems necessary to say that managerial appraisal should measure *performance* as a *manager* in meeting goals for which the manager is responsible. Yet obvious as this is, or at least should be, examination of a large number of appraisal systems used by business, government, and other enterprises shows a lack of understanding of this truism,

or at least an unwillingness or inability to translate understanding into practice.

Note then that appraisal should measure both *performance*
in accomplishing goals and plans and *performance as a
manager.* No one would want a person in a managerial role
who appeared to do everything right as a manager but who
could not turn in a good record of profit making, marketing,
controllership, or whatever his area of responsibility might
be. Nor should one be satisfied to have a performer in a
managerial position who cannot operate effectively as a
manager. Performers tend to be "flashes in the pan" and
many are the performers who have succeeded in spite of
themselves.

Performance in Accomplishing Goals   In assessing performance,
the newer systems of appraising against verifiable preselected goals, dealt with in detail in Chapters 3 and 4, represent the best systems that have yet been devised. Given
consistent, integrated, and understood planning designed
to reach verifiable goals, the best criteria of the manager are
his goals (including the intelligence with which he makes
them), the planning programs he devises to accomplish them,
and his success in achieving them. Those who have operated
under some variation of this system have often claimed that
this is adequate and that elements of luck or other factors
beyond the manager's control are taken into account in
arriving at any appraisal. To some extent this may be true.
But there are too many cases of the sparkling performer being
promoted despite these factors and the performing failure
being inaccurately blamed.

Performance as Managers   Although an impressive record
of setting and accomplishing goals is persuasive evidence
of any group leader's ability, it is proposed in this book to
supplement this standard of performance by an appraisal of
a manager *as a manager.* One must grant that a manager at

any level undertakes nonmanagerial duties, and these cannot be overlooked. The primary purpose for which a manager is hired, and against which he should be measured, however, is his performance as a manager. This should indicate that he be appraised on the basis of how well he understands and undertakes the managerial functions of planning, organizing, staffing, directing, and controlling. For standards in this area we must turn to the fundamentals of management.

Requirements for an Effective Appraisal System

There are a few requirements for any program of managerial appraisal to be effective. Anyone who would like to analyze his own system would do well to weigh it against these criteria.

1. *The Program Should Measure the Right Things.* As pointed out above, the effective program must weigh both a manager's performance in accomplishing goals for which he is responsible and his performance as a manager.

It is entirely possible, also, that an evaluator might wish to measure a manager's expertise in nonmanagerial skills and knowledge. Is he a perceptive and imaginative developer of marketing programs if he is a marketing manager? If he is a research laboratory director, can he give his group technical leadership and act as a communications link between non-technically oriented fellow or superior managers?

A manager who does well on an appraisal of performance against objectives and performance as a manager is likely to look good on the nonmanagerial aspects of his job. In order to plan, operate, and control well, he may find expertise in his functional field a very important adjunct to his abilities. Nevertheless, he will probably find that to do the best job he must usually rely on others. Assuring himself that a network of verifiable goals and plans exists, that the organization structure establishes the right system of roles, that these roles are well manned, that he leads and directs with understanding and assistance to subordinates, and that he and his subordinates know how well they are doing and take action to correct deviations from plans, all these things—the basic functions of the manager—should go far to mobilize expertise for results in nonmanagerial areas.

2. *The Program Should Be Operational.* The most effective appraisal program will not be one that is an exercise separate from the operations of the individual manager. It must be operational in the sense that appraisal is an activity of merely looking at what people are doing. Unlike the long-used system of appraising individuals on the basis of their personality traits, work habits, or their ability to get along with others, the effective appraisal program is integrated with work and results.

This is why a combination of appraisal of performance against verifiable goals and performance as a manager is to be preferred over other appraisal programs. Both of these are operational. They tie in with and reflect the manager on his job. They are not separate from it.

3. *The Program Should Be Objective.* Any appraisal program gains as it becomes more objective. Both those who appraise and those being appraised prefer objectivity. A manager who must weigh people on the basis of what he "thinks" of them understandably shies away from accurate appraisal and is likely to give people ratings—usually too high—that cannot be challenged by the person being rated. People being appraised understandably tend to resent subjective criticism as not being fair.

The key to objectivity in goal performance is verifiability, the quality that makes it possible to ascertain whether or not a given goal has or has not been accomplished. While goals expressed in quantitative terms—dollars of profit or percentage of cost reduction—are the most verifiable, goals stated in qualitative terms—a program with certain characteristics to be completed by a certain date—are also verifiable.

Making objectives verifiable and appraising results against them have gone far to remove the subjective element from evaluation. The subjective element has not been completely removed, however, as will be pointed out in Chapter 4. Nor have elements of subjectivity been eliminated from the program proposed here to evaluate managers as managers. Indeed, there are few, if any, programs of evaluation in any area—university grades, drivers' tests, selecting football all-Americans, and others—where we have succeeded in obtaining complete objectivity. But this does not mean that our eyes should be shut to the hope that better and more objective systems of evaluation may be developed.

4. *The Program Should Be Acceptable.* Any management technique or program that people will not accept is likely to be ineffective. If forced to, people will give lip service to programs and fill out forms. However, if they understand and believe in a program and see it as a means of helping accomplish their own personal desires through contributing to group goals, in other words if they accept it, they will use it and feel a sense of commitment to the program.

A primary factor in acceptance is whether the program is understood. One of the characteristics of Homo sapiens is that what he does not understand, he tends to distrust, and what he does not trust, he will not effectively use. One of the major failures of many management programs is due to this factor. Sometimes misunderstanding arises from lack of indoctrination and explanation. Sometimes it is due to complexity. This, in turn, is a relative matter, depending on the degree of sophistication of the persons involved.

Many are the management programs—variable budgeting, network analyses (PERT/CPM), rate-of-return-on-investment analysis, and management appraisals—that are based on sound principles but fail because of lack of understanding and undue complexity. Wise is the management consultant, executive, or staff specialist who will gear a program, even though it be a relatively crude approach, to the level of sophistication of those who must operate it.

Another factor in acceptance is the existence of continuing top- and middle-management support. Many sound programs have been successfully launched only to fail because of executive malnutrition.

Acceptance and understanding are partners in the ability of subordinates to see in a program a means of achieving self-actualization, as well as fulfilling the more prosaic requirements such as success, appreciation, promotion, and compensation. These are prerequisites to commitment, a feeling of obligation and a desire to accomplish.

5. *The Program Should Be Constructive.* The effective managerial appraisal program should be constructive in the sense that it will help individuals to improve their abilities and work. The purpose of an appraisal, of course, is not only to determine how well an individual meets job requirements, as important as this is. It should do more. By pointing to his errors, weaknesses, or failures, it should provide him with a learning experience. An effective appraisal program will do this.

chapter two

The Nature and Deficiencies of Traditional Appraisal Systems

If the criteria for an effective appraisal system outlined in the previous chapter can be accepted, it is easy to see how traditional appraisal systems have usually missed their target. Some of this has been due to the fact that relatively little has been known about managing and its underlying science until recent years. Even now, what is known is fairly crude and embryonic. Some of this arises from the fact that managing is a highly complex art involving technical, economic, and cultural variables that are not only very numerous but often difficult to comprehend. What has happened, also, is that too little research and inventiveness have been applied to appraisals, as indeed to virtually every aspect of managing.

Perhaps some light may be cast by looking at the history of appraisal and at traditional appraisal systems. The traditional approach has been to judge people on personality or activity traits. After predictable dissatisfaction with this basis of appraisal, a number of attempts have been made over the years to repair its deficiencies. But not until this approach has been abandoned, as is increasingly becoming the case, will meaningful progress be made toward effective appraisal.

The Development of Managerial Appraisal

References to appraisal of managers can be found in antiquity. It is reported that emperors of the Wei dynasty (A.D. 221–265) had an "Imperial Rater" whose task it was to evaluate the performance of the official family. Centuries later, Ignatius Loyola established a system for formal rating of the members of the Jesuit Society.[1]

Perhaps the first use of formal appraisal in the United States was in systems used by the federal government and certain city administrators in the latter part of the nineteenth century, a move induced by criticism of waste and the spoils system in government. The real impetus to appraisal in business came as the result of the work measurement programs of Frederick Taylor and his followers before World War I. It was natural that these early appraisal programs would be related to various numerical efficiency factors developed from work simplification and time and motion study. Likewise, with widespread awareness of human relations factors in managing in the early 1930's and 1940's, it is understandable that behavioral traits, such as "ability to get along with others," would tend to become dominant in appraisal systems.

[1] These references are from T. L. Whisler and S. F. Harper (eds.), *Performance Appraisal: Research and Practice* (New York: Holt, Rinehart and Winston, Inc., 1962), p. 423.

Early appraisal systems were almost inevitably aimed at evaluation of hourly workers rather than managers. The trouble with most managerial performance appraisal systems, largely introduced during World War II and immediately thereafter, is that they apparently had their foundations in hourly labor performance appraisals. Too many of these, in turn, were based on worker qualities and attitudes and on aspects of cooperation and conformity, rather than on performance. Thus, in a typical employee rating report, the supervisor was asked to rate, primarily in subjective terms, such things as quality of work, quantity of work, adaptability, job knowledge, dependability, housekeeping, safety, and cooperative attitude.

Even at the hourly worker level, such subjective kinds of evaluations do tend to force the supervisor to judge people with little real evidence or few meaningful standards. At the level of managerial performance, they become virtually untenable. It is no wonder that, with such approaches to evaluation, we find much that is true in the criticism of conformity and "togetherness" made so famous by William Whyte in his stimulating book *The Organization Man*.

The Traditional Trait Approach

Although there are many variations in practice, traditional appraisals have been based on weighing traits of individuals and general characteristics of their work. Dissatisfaction with the accuracy and credibility of trait evaluations has led to many attempts to repair perceived deficiencies, but even these, as will be noted later, have been based on general characteristics of people and performance that cannot easily be made verifiable or objective, if at all.

The typical trait-rating evaluation system in use for many years by companies and government agencies might list ten to fifteen traits or personal characteristics, such as ability to get along with people, leadership, analytical ability, industry, judgment, initiative, and so forth. In evaluating a manager on each count, the rater could choose one of five or six ratings ranging from unacceptable to outstanding.

A typical trait-oriented appraisal is that used by the United States Navy for many years in appraising officers. While the "Report on the Fitness of Officers" required information on duties and study courses carried out, questioned whether the reviewing officer desired to have the subordinate in his command, and had a provision for open-ended comments, the major portion of the evaluation was involved in the trait analysis shown in Table 1.

While the number and exact nature of traits utilized by a given organization might vary, traditional appraisal systems have generally emphasized predominantly psychological factors. In one study, made in 1957, it was concluded that:

> Most companies, it appears from a study of appraisal blanks, are concerned mainly with personality and character traits. . . . So strongly is the emphasis on personality that "job knowledge" and even "job performance" may have only a minor place in the overall rating.[2]

One expert believes we have "drifted" into the trait approach for three reasons.[3] In the first place, as the behavioral sciences have captured increased public interest, we have become more prone to try to explain effectiveness by psychological or psychiatric measures. Second, since so many managerial tasks cannot be given quantitative measurement and since qualitative factors are difficult to measure, we have tended to drift toward personality-centered appraisals.

[2] Ernest Dale and Alice Smith, "Now Report Cards for Bosses," *New York Times Magazine,* Mar. 31, 1957.

[3] Philip R. Kelly, "Reappraisal of Appraisals," *Harvard Business Review,* vol. 36, no. 3, p. 60 (May–June, 1958).

TABLE 1 Qualities and Rating Form of U.S. Navy Report on Fitness of Officers

	NOT OBSERVED	OUTSTANDING	EXCELLENT	AVERAGE	UNSATIS-FACTORY
(a) INTELLIGENCE (With reference to the faculty of comprehension; mental acuteness.)		Exceptionally quick-witted; keen in understanding.	Grasps essentials of a situation quickly.	Understands normal situations and conditions.	
(b) JUDGMENT (With reference to a discriminating perception by which the values and relations of things are mentally asserted.)		Unusually keen in estimating situations and reaching sound decisions.	Can generally be depended on to make proper decisions.	Fair judgment in normal and routine things.	
(c) INITIATIVE (With reference to constructive thinking and resourcefulness; ability and intelligence to act on own responsibility.)		Exceptional in ability to think, plan, and do things without waiting to be told and instructed.	Able to plan and execute missions on his own responsibility.	Capable of performing routine duties on own responsibility.	
(d) FORCE (With reference to moral power possessed and exerted in producing results.)		Strong, dynamic.	Strong.	Effectual under normal and routine circumstances.	
(e) LEADERSHIP (With reference to the faculty of directing, controlling, and influencing others in definite lines of action and of maintaining discipline.)		Inspires others to a high degree by precept and example. Requires a high standard of discipline.	A very good leader.	Leads fairly well.	
(f) MORAL COURAGE (With reference to that mental quality which impels one to carry out the dictates of his conscience and convictions fearlessly.)		Exceptionally courageous.	Courageous to a high degree.	Fairly courageous.	
(g) COOPERATION (With reference to the faculty of working harmoniously with others toward the accomplishment of common duties.)		Exceptionally successful in working with others to a common end.	Works in harmony with others.	Cooperates fairly well.	

A MARK TO THE RIGHT OF THIS LINE CONST

(h) LOYALTY (Fidelity, faithfulness, allegiance, constancy—all with reference to a cause and to higher authority.)		Unswerving in allegiance; frank and honest in aiding and advising.	A high sense of loyalty.	Reasonably faithful in the execution of his duty.
(i) PERSEVERANCE (With reference to maintenance of purpose or undertaking in spite of obstacles or discouragement.)		Determined, resolute.	Constant in purpose.	Fairly steady.
(j) REACTION IN EMERGENCIES (With reference to the faculty of acting instinctively in a logical manner in difficult and unforeseen situations.)		Exceptionally cool-headed and logical in his actions under all conditions.	Composed and logical in his actions in difficult situations.	Fairly logical in his actions in general.
(k) ENDURANCE (With reference to ability for carrying on under any and all conditions.)		Capable of standing an exceptional amount of physical hardship and strain.	Can perform well his duties under trying conditions.	Of normal endurance.
(l) INDUSTRY (With reference to performance of duties in an energetic manner.)		Extremely energetic and industrious.	Thorough and energetic.	Reasonably energetic and industrious.
(m) MILITARY BEARING AND NEATNESS OF PERSON AND DRESS (With reference to dignity of demeanor, correctness of uniform, and smartness of appearance.)		Exceptional.	Very good.	Fair.

14. A report containing adverse matter must be referred to the officer reported on for statement pursuant to article 1701 (8) USNR. His statement should be attached to this report. Statements of minor deficiencies either in character or performance of duties must be brought to the attention of the officer reported on either orally or in writing.

HAS THIS BEEN DONE?_____WHAT IMPROVEMENT, IF ANY, HAS BEEN NOTED?_____

_____

_____

_____(Signature of reporting senior)_____

21

A third factor relates to the manager's job; practically every study has found successful managers to be strong leaders and has highlighted human relations skills.

Major Deficiencies of Trait Appraisals

Experience has shown that trait appraisals suffer from great deficiencies. Managers resist doing them or tend to go through the paper work without knowing exactly how to rate. Even where earnest attempts have been made to "sell" such programs, to indoctrinate managers, and to train them in the meaning of traits so that they can improve their appraisal ability, few managers can or will do them well.

The author can remember, when he was in an executive position, being asked to evaluate his subordinate managers on a list of typical traits. He put it off as long as he could because he did not want to rate subordinates as he saw them since he knew he could not prove his rating. Then, when the personnel manager made life so miserable that he could delay no longer, he took the forms home one evening and rated all of them "excellent" or "outstanding"—which they were not.

One practical problem of the trait approach to appraisal is that, because trait evaluation cannot be objective, serious fair-minded managers do not wish to utilize their obviously subjective judgment on a matter as important as performance. And employees who receive less than the top rating almost invariably feel that they have been unfairly dealt with. This "playing with people's souls" may be the province of the professional psychiatrist, but hardly that of the manager.

Another problem is that the basic assumption of trait appraisals is open to question. The connection between performance and possession of traits is doubtful. It also tends to be outside of, separated from, a manager's actual operations. It substitutes what someone *thinks* of an individual for what he actually *does*. This is made even more constraining when we find in trait appraisal forms too few references to the actual job being done.

The results of resistance by managers are several. Many look upon it as only a paper-work exercise that must be done because someone has ordered it. When this happens, people go through the paper work and tend to make ratings as painless (for the subordinate and the manager) as possible. Consequently, they tend not to be very discriminating. It is interesting, but hardly surprising, that a study of ratings of Navy officers a few years ago came up with an arithmetic paradox: that of all officers of the U.S. Navy rated over a period of time, some 98.5 percent were outstanding or excellent and only 1 percent were average!

Trait criteria are at best nebulous. Raters are dealing with a blunt tool and subordinates are likely to be vague about what it is they are being rated on. Since raters are painfully aware that in the hands of most practitioners it is a crude device, they are reluctant to use it in a manner which would affect the careers of their subordinates. One of the principal purposes of appraisal is to provide a basis upon which to discuss performance and plan for improvement. But trait evaluations provide little tangible to discuss, little on which participants can agree as fact, and therefore little mutual understanding of what would be required to obtain improvement.

Even when the mere ticking off of boxes to give a fast and effortless rating is supplemented by requiring that comments be made by raters, the results are often not much more encouraging. Managers who have to go through this a number of times tend to develop a lexicon of phrases which are useful but not always discriminating. An extreme example of some of these phrases and their humorous results was reported by an anonymous U.S. Air Force officer as follows:[4]

> This officer has talents but has kept them well hidden. He has failed to demonstrate any outstanding weaknesses. Never makes the same mistake twice but it seems to me that he has made them all once.
> A quiet, reticent, neat appearing officer—industrious, tenacious, diffident, careful, and neat. I do not wish to have this officer as a member of my command at any time.
> An independent thinker with a mediocre mentality.

In view of its deficiencies, one is surprised to find a trait-oriented appraisal system still so widely used. Even as it has been improved in technique, approach, and content, it still has questionable practical validity.

Attempts to Strengthen the Content of the Trait Approach

As the deficiencies of trait approaches have been recognized, a number of changes and additions have been introduced. Some are aimed at making the traits more comprehensible to raters; some have attempted to force better and more discriminating appraisal; some have softened the personality bias by bringing in other appraisal factors; and, particularly in recent years, the trend has been toward emphasizing key results but still in a generalized way. The more generally used modifications will be dealt with briefly.

Explaining Traits   For some years now, attempts have aimed at making trait appraisal effective by concentrating on explaining the meaning of various traits and interpreting degrees of perfection or imperfection. This is illustrated by

---

[4] Reported in Whisler and Harper, *op. cit.,* p. 221.

the U.S. Navy "Report on the Fitness of Officers" in Table 1. Instead of merely saying "judgment," the report defines this quality as "discriminating perception by which values and relations to things are mentally asserted." An "excellent" rating is one where the person being rated "can generally be depended on to make proper decisions."

In a form of a well-known business corporation, similar explanations were made. For example, it defined "judgment" as "how capable is he in recognizing the significant from the less significant in arriving at sound conclusions?" In turn, a top rating in this and other areas would be based on the criterion of "he stands out as being among the best you have known" and a "satisfactory" rating would be based on "he fulfills essential requirements."

In another trait appraisal form, judgment is grouped with "judgment, common sense, and initiative" and this quality is defined as "ability to proceed with his job without being told every detail, to make suggestions, to solve problems, to be generally resourceful." Various degrees of this quality vary from the highest—"sound judgment and high degree of resourcefulness at all times"—to the lowest—"judgment can't be relied on; shows no initiative."

As can be seen, even attempts to explain traits and degrees of effectiveness are subject to generalities, words that are difficult to construe in practice and carry varying degrees of interpretation. In essence they are still subjective in nature, reflecting what the rater *thinks* of a man rather than what he is or does. They also can hardly be translated into action for improvement or promotion with a significant degree of accuracy.

Adding Work-oriented Qualities   Early in the use of trait appraisals, personality factors far outweighed work performance factors. By the mid-1950's, however, virtually every trait type of appraisal used, at least for managers, had added a number of work-oriented qualities.

For example, in one of the appraisal forms used by a well-known company, organizational ability is appraised with the questions: "How successful is he in arranging the total activity into logical, practical assignments?" and "To what extent does he develop personnel so that they are effective in their assignments?" Likewise, in control, "To what extent does he see that plans and instructions are carried out?" As can be seen, such questions as these do bear directly on a man's managerial ability although they suffer from being somewhat too broad and giving too few checkpoints.

Others have emphasized performance factors. In one form, for example, all performance except personal traits and managerial qualities was summarized under "results on job," and this was defined as "results he obtains in terms of production, cost, and quality." Another performance criterion sometimes used is the degree of budget accomplishment, with the top rating of "performs within budget even under severe circumstances" to the bottom rating of "almost always misses budgets and deviations are substantial."

Typical of the more advanced trait and quality appraisal form is that in Table 2. It will be readily noted that this form has traits covering personality, knowledge and experience, and work, as well as qualities of managing and a few dealing with work performance. It also does a fairly good job of explaining what is meant by traits and qualities and various degrees of grading. However, it suffers from the disability of being almost entirely subjective.

Open-ended Appraisals There have been a number of appraisal programs which can be called "open-end" performance evaluations. In these the appraiser is not asked to rate on a basis of a list of personality traits or work qualities. Instead he is asked to supply whatever evidence on performance he feels is pertinent for appraisal. He may be given a broad outline to consider, such as performance in "operations," "organization," "personnel," and "financial," and he may be asked specifically to consider such things as quality, quantity, and time element of work, or customer relations and subordinate employee morale.

Truly open-ended appraisals have seldom been found to be satisfactory because the results were often too general and not adequately discriminating. Also, after a few rounds of this appraisal approach, raters soon found it advantageous to have a ready list of "canned" comments that could be inserted, usually meaninglessly, into the spaces provided.

Open-ended with Position Description Guidelines   The weakness of the open-ended approach has been the lack of guidelines. Some companies gave some meaning to this approach by tying it to a manager's position description. Taking every element of the position description as a checkpoint, the rater comments on the effectiveness with which the duties spelled out are being performed.

Assuming the position description is fairly accurate and up to date and the major duties are properly highlighted, which is not always the case, this approach places emphasis on the job. Thus it moves in the right direction of measuring what a man should do and how he does it. But it is still open to question as to how objective the evaluation can be unless the required duties are translated into a series of verifiable performance standards.

Key Result Areas   Closely related to utilizing position descriptions and appraisal against verifiable objectives of which they are the precursor, key result areas have been spelled out as standards of appraisal, replacing traits and qualities. The starting point for selection of key result areas is usually

TABLE 2 Typical Advanced Trait and Work Rating Form for Managerial Personnel

	EXCELLENT	GOOD	AVERAGE	FAIR	POOR
1. KNOWLEDGE OF JOB Familiarity with the various procedures of the work	Exceptional mastery of all phases of his work	Thorough knowledge of practically all phases of his work	Adequate knowledge of particular job	Insufficient knowledge of some phases of job	Inadequate comprehension of requirements of job
2. EXPERIENCE Skill and practical wisdom gained by personal knowledge	Broad background and training for particular job	A comprehensive background	An adequate background	Has some background but requires direction	Inexperienced or unsatisfactory progress
3. GENERAL COMPANY INFORMATION Knowledge of major and minor company policies	Thorough understanding and appreciation of all company policies	Knowledge of practically all company policies	Acceptable knowledge of company policies	Limited knowledge of company policies	Does not have enough information to be efficient
4. HEALTH Soundness of body and mind, and freedom from physical disease or disability	Robust, energetic	Sufficiently healthy and energetic to handle the job	Sufficiently healthy to handle job but not overly energetic	Frail, affected by pressure	Sickly. Affects his work
5. ENTHUSIASM A positive, ardent, and eager response	Believes wholeheartedly in the company and expresses both orally and in his attitude that belief	Works enthusiastically, not too expressive	Matter-of-fact attitude	Definitely passive or indifferent	Negative in attitude
6. PERSONALITY The external mannerisms consciously or unconsciously adopted in meeting situations	Radiant, confident, poised, courteous	Pleasant, forceful	Likeable	Ill at ease, not too forceful	Negative colorless person
7. APPEARANCE Outward impressions made by a person	Superior style, grooming, taste and a sense of the fitness of things	Well dressed and neat	Neat, but not particularly striking	Intermittently careless	Slovenly and untidy
8. CHARACTER Integrity of an individual	Has the courage of his convictions and unquestioned habits	Morally sound. Tolerant	An average human being possessing average personal weaknesses	A person whose behavior harms no one but himself	A person who is a bad influence on the behavior of the group
9. MENTALITY Quality of mind, mental power, and creative intellectual ability of a person	Superior ability to think clearly and arrive at sound conclusions	Worthwhile ideas of his own, and ability to make useful decisions	Well informed on certain subjects useful in his daily work	Little ability to comprehend, interpret or grasp new ideas	Unable to reason logically
10. SOCIABILITY Sense of mutual relationship, companionship, and friendliness with others	A genuine interest in people and extremely well liked by others	A friendly, pleasant person, happy in a group	Willing to be a part of a group but makes little contribution	Poorly adjusted to the group	Unwilling to be a part of any group activities
11. ABILITY TO GET THINGS DONE Ability to perform, execute, and achieve an assigned task	Completes assignments in the shortest possible time	Completes assignments in unusually short time	Completes assignments in a reasonable time	Slow in completing assignments, or does not complete them	Takes a long time to accomplish little
12. COOPERATIVE An appreciation of collective action for mutual profit or common benefit	Greatest possible cooperativeness	Very cooperative	Cooperative	Difficult to handle	Obstructive
13. ACCEPTANCE OF RESPONSIBILITY Willingness to assume duties	Greatest possible sense of responsibility	Very willing	Accepts but does not seek responsibility	Does assigned tasks reluctantly	Irresponsible

	EXCELLENT	GOOD	AVERAGE	FAIR	POOR
14. JUDGMENT Ability to grasp a situation and draw correct conclusions	☐ Superior ability to think intelligently and use sound judgment	☐ Excellent judgment	☐ Good common sense	☐ Poor judgment	☐ Neglects and misinterprets the facts
15. INITIATIVE Desire and ability to introduce a new course of action	☐ Seeks and sets for himself additional tasks, highly ingenious	☐ Very resourceful	☐ Progressive	☐ Rarely suggests	☐ Needs detailed instruction
16. EXPRESSION Ability to articulate and orally express one's thoughts and feelings	☐ Unusually articulate in expressing thoughts and feelings; master of good speech techniques	☐ Speaks well	☐ Nothing about his speech that is distinctive or distasteful	☐ Careless speech habits and mild physical defects	☐ Inarticulate and physical defects
17. RATE OF WORK The time taken to finish a specific assignment	☐ Greatest possible rapidity	☐ Very rapid	☐ Good speed	☐ Slow	☐ Hopelessly slow
18. ACCURACY A high percentage of freedom from mistakes	☐ Highest possible accuracy	☐ Very careful	☐ Careful, no more than reasonable time required for revision	☐ Careless, time required for revision greatly excessive	☐ Practically worthless work
19. BUDGET ACCOMPLISHMENT	☐ Performs within budget even under severe circumstances	☐ Performance almost within budget. Deviations.	☐ Performs within budget more than two-thirds of the time and seldom are deviations substantial	☐ Misses budget frequently and deviations are substantial	☐ Almost always misses budget and deviations are often substantial
20. CONDITION OF DEPARTMENT	☐ Extremely orderly	☐ Very orderly	☐ No particular disorder	☐ Disorderliness in department	☐ Department very disorderly
21. HANDLING PEOPLE The ability to appreciate, understand, and direct individual differences	☐ Extremely successful in helping and training his men to progress and attain their ambitions	☐ Capable leader	☐ Fails to develop and obtain maximum results from men	☐ Fails to command confidence	☐ Antagonizes his subordinates
22. DEVELOPING ASSISTANTS The ability to delegate responsibilities to the right individual	☐ Superior ability in selecting suitable men and training them to assume specific responsibilities	☐ Very capable in recognizing and training subordinates	☐ Good in selection, but little attention is given to training	☐ Allows subordinates to shift for themselves	☐ Hinders the natural development of his men
23. DELEGATING WORK The assignment of specific responsibilities	☐ Superior ability in recognizing individual's capacities, when he assigns tasks	☐ Capable supervisor	☐ Fails to recognize individual's capacities	☐ Fails to see work to be done	☐ Does all the work himself
24. PLANNING AND ORGANIZING Success in organizing, by delegating authority and planning	☐ Highest possible effectiveness	☐ Effective under difficult situations	☐ Effective under normal circumstances	☐ Lacks planning ability	☐ Inefficient
25. VISION The power to see and imagine	☐ Superior ability to think creatively, foresee and imagine	☐ Very capable in anticipating the future	☐ Ability to plan in advance	☐ Overly realistic	☐ Devoid of imagination
26. SELLING COMPANY POLICIES Company loyalty and an eagerness to tell others	☐ An extremely loyal employee eager to express to outsiders his enthusiasm	☐ A very loyal employee	☐ Passive in his attitude toward Company policies	☐ Critical of all Company policies	☐ Disloyal and traitorous

Signature of Rater _____

the organization chart and position descriptions, although key result areas can be developed through discussion and consensus of the manager and his superior.

For example, one would find that the key results expected from a controller might include:

1. Presenting sound forecasts for budget making, tempering his judgment with estimates of the sales and manufacturing departments.

2. Working with appropriate division and department heads to assemble a coordinated budget for presentation to the executive committee.

3. Maintaining careful review of balance-sheet ratios to help anticipate financial needs and plans.

4. Helping establish sound pricing policies.

5. Keeping credit losses to a minimum.

6. Policing inventory control, credit position, and budget adherence of departments.

7. Maintaining accurate accounts, billings, and payments, taking full advantage of electronic data-processing equipment.

Another approach is based on setting up key results as fairly specific standards. Some companies take up each portion of a manager's position description and then define it in terms of results expected when performance is satisfactory. For example, a prominent bank set up performance for branch managers in this way, and a portion of the key results are as follows:[5]

I. *Business Development*. The solicitation of business from noncustomers and the development and promotion of additional business from present customers.

Performance is satisfactory when:
a. Business development calls are intelligently scheduled and

[5] Taken from J. W. Enell and G. H. Haas, *Setting Standards for Executive Performance* (New York: American Management Association, 1960), pp. 251–253.

well planned, including acquiring a knowledge of the prospects' business.

b. Patience and perseverance are displayed in business development contacts, especially on prospects.

c. Manager possesses adequate knowledge of all the Bank's services.

d. Manager keeps informed about the banking business and the particular appeal of its services.

e. Customers are kept well informed regarding all services the Bank can render to them.

f. Manager is alert to the changing needs and required services of the Bank's customers.

g. Manager is alert to and keeps staff informed of —
   (1) General economic conditions.
   (2) Changing business conditions in the area.
   (3) Competitors' aims, activities, and services.
   (4) Opportunities for business development.

II. *Customer Relations.* Provide branch banking services to a community in a manner superior to that which could be provided by our competitors.

Performance is satisfactory when:

a. There is evidence that manager is alert to customers' needs and is qualified to serve them.

b. Manager displays sincere interest in customers' accounts and problems.

c. All banking relationships are held strictly confidential.

d. Customers are kept well informed of bank policies.

e. Manager is well informed on commercial and savings account activity.

III. *Loan Processing.* The process of eliciting necessary facts through personal customer interview, accepting loan applications, and following through to completion on such applications to enable lending officers to expedite extension of credit to qualified individuals.

Performance is satisfactory when:

a. There is evidence of adequate basic knowledge of the lending function.

b. Individual has demonstrated clear knowledge of loan-processing procedures.

c. Individual has displayed ability to obtain necessary facts in a commercial loan interview; uses initiative and independent action when necessary to decline obviously unqualified applicants without impairing customer good will.

d. There is evidence that customers place confidence in individual's ability to satisfy their loan requirements.

e. Lending officer does not generally find it necessary to overrule individual's judgment.

f. There is evidence that individual has actually processed and completed loan transactions without experiencing difficulty.

IV. *Branch Administration.* Manages or directs Branch affairs so as to insure that the specific activities necessary to achieve branch objectives are carried out.

Performance is satisfactory when:

a. Planning. There is evidence that he looks ahead and visualizes and assesses specific conditions, both within the Branch and externally, which will confront him in the near future as well as over a longer period. Ascertains that work is planned and goals are set in accordance with plans. Identifies in concrete terms what he expects his group to accomplish, and follows through to see goals have been reached.

b. Organization. Delegates to subordinates as much as possible of the work to be done, reserving for his own performance only that management work which cannot be effectively performed by subordinates.

c. Coordination. Works to create harmonious relationships among all positions so that all members of his Branch can work effectively together toward their common goal.

d. Motivation. Encourages staff to work at highest productivity by creating a climate in the office favorable to individual and group accomplishment.

e. Control. Adopts a systematic means of reviewing operations to determine whether the results he expects are being accomplished, and takes corrective action in terms of exceptions noted.

V. *Delegation.* The process of assigning responsibility with commensurate authority so that work and personnel functions will be performed most effectively.

Performance is satisfactory when:

a. There is evidence of planning for appropriate delegation of responsibility.
   (1) Before delegating, the Manager reviews with his management personnel the organization of the Branch.
   (2) He reviews management appraisals.
b. Subordinates are informed of and understand their responsibilities and authorities (appraisal interview).
c. Subordinates are permitted to exercise fully the duties outlined in job descriptions.
d. There are indications that subordinates are being assigned additional responsibilities to develop their individual capabilities.
e. Manager keeps aware of and control over Branch matters without burdening himself with unnecessary detail.
f. Branch operates efficiently in presence and absence of manager.

VI. *Effective Use of Manpower.* The process of determining when, where, and by whom a given job will be performed and time required to complete it.

Performance is satisfactory when:
a. The skills of employees are utilized to improve service and to lower costs.
b. Manager is alert to possibilities for improving customer service and internal branch methods.
c. Manager cooperates with Branch Department and Main Office in improvement of operating procedures, traffic surveys, etc.
d. Procedures are used to quickly locate and correct faulty service.
e. Exempt employees are not performing routine and non-exempt work.
f. Work is planned for maximum use of equipment.
g. Work is planned for maximum use of personnel.

VII. *Communications.* The process of interchanging information, ideas, and opinions so that the Branch can be operated most effectively.

Performance is satisfactory when:
a. The Branch Department is kept informed (for example) on:
   (1) Personnel matters.

      (2) Status of customer service.

      (3) Performance of subordinates.

    b. Staff meetings are being conducted.

      (1) General staff meetings.

      (2) Brief special meetings.

      (3) Management meetings.

    c. There is evidence of voluntary and free consultation or contact between the Branch Manager and his subordinates, and between the Branch Manager and the Branch Department.

    d. There is evidence of good relations and high morale within the Branch.

There can be no question that relating appraisal to position description duties and further refining it by developing standards of satisfactory performance against these duties represent a massive step away from traditional appraisal by traits or work qualities. This properly places emphasis on performance, where it should be, rather than on personality. It goes some distance in reducing vagueness and subjectivity. It puts appraisal in a frame of reference that managers can and will understand.

But there are still far too many general terms like "adequate," "help," "minimum," "maximum," "intelligently," "sincere interest," "well informed," "clear," "good," and "high." These and similar adjectives are simply not verifiable. They still reflect too much what a rater "thinks" rather than what a person being rated does. They do, however, become a first step toward making performance objectives verifiable.

Attempts to Improve the Effectiveness of the Rating Process

Because of the failure of raters to exercise enough thoroughness and discrimination in rating, a number of techniques have been utilized to improve effectiveness of the rating process. Some deal with the way the rating is done and others tend to force the rater to be more discriminating.

Subordinate and Superior Rating   In many rating systems it is provided that the subordinate being rated appraise himself on the same form and at the same time the superior appraises him. Then, after each has made a rating, the two compare their appraisals and explain differences.

For any rating system this technique has much to commend it. It forces the subordinate to make an appraisal of himself and the kind of job he is doing. It also alerts him to the elements on which the superior will be making his rating and thereby prepares him for his superior's rating. It furthermore tends to eliminate some of the distance between the rater and the rated and makes the evaluation more of a cooperative process.

Combining self-rating with rating by the superior gives people a better understanding of the appraisal process, the factors and standards of measurement, and what is expected of them in their job. It likewise forces consideration of differences and the airing of grievances and obstructions to performance. By removing some of the mystery of rating, it is likely to cause greater appreciation of appraisals.

Some superiors resist having their subordinates do self-appraisals and then compare notes with them. As a result, self-appraisals are often made voluntary. But where a fairly good program of evaluation exists and where the rater takes his obligation seriously, the resultant understanding and removal of the boss from an Olympian pedestal give rise to a closeness and a constructive atmosphere that cannot be easily obtained in any other way. While there is something to be said for leaving self-appraisal voluntary, there is much more in favor of strongly encouraging it. Companies who have done so report success in joint appraisal in at least 95 percent of the cases.

As a matter of fact, if people understand the appraisal system, they tend to enjoy self-appraisal. Experience has disclosed, too, that subordinates are remarkably objective about themselves. It has also fairly generally shown that good managers tend to be more critical of themselves than their boss is, although poorer ones may often overrate themselves. Moreover, experience with self-evaluation gives persuasive evidence that it encourages self-development.

Having the Superior's Superior Participate in Rating   Effectiveness of evaluation has also been enhanced by having the superior's superior participate in rating. This may be done in either of two ways: (1) by having the immediate superior of the rater independently evaluate the latter's subordinate, or (2) by having the superior's superior review the rater's appraisal. Then the two get together to explain or reconcile any differences.

In either event, the result will almost surely be a more objective and thorough appraisal. It also gives the higher manager an insight into the managerial abilities of the men reporting to him, helps him in guiding them, and brings directly to his attention the weaknesses and strengths of the second echelon below him. Doing so is likely also to give a better picture up the line on the accuracy, adequacy, and effectiveness of the management appraisal program being used and also of any management development program.

In any case, whether an appraisal program is soundly based or not and whether it utilizes traits and qualities or verifiable objectives, the superior's superior's review is highly desirable. It means work, takes time, and requires some visibility. But it is difficult to comprehend an activity much more important. A president of one of the nation's largest firms told the author that he and the chairman spent approximately one-third of their time on such appraisal activities.

Peer Rating and Subordinate Rating   Many specialists have recommended that an individual be rated not only by his superiors but by his peers and his subordinates. There is much to be said for this approach. Peers and subordinates are likely to have a clearer view of a manager than his superiors. This is particularly true of the inept managers who can often "snow" their superiors by subservient bootlicking and by excuses which a superior—with his almost inevitable paternalism toward those who report to him—is too likely to accept.

But in the author's experience and observation, peer and subordinate ratings seldom work as intended. The natural tendency to do some logrolling and mutual "backscratching" and the fear that criticism will produce retaliation when it becomes the rater's turn to be evaluated have weakened the effectiveness of peer rating. Subordinates are also normally fearful of being objective or honest about their superior because they realize the tremendous power he has over their economic security and future. Moreover, incompetent subordinates tolerated by a superior are not likely to be very objective about their boss, nor are troublemakers with an axe to grind.

Group Rating   A few organizations follow a system of group rating. Sometimes the group is one of peers and is subject to the deficiencies outlined above. In other cases it may be a group of managers and staff specialists on the level of the superior undertaking the rating.

The ordinary process is to have individuals from departments and staff positions who have had occasion to work with the person to be evaluated. Each of them makes an independent appraisal, and then they meet and consolidate their results. Sometimes they use the appraisal forms of the company system. In other cases, the appraisers approach the job with a few sheets of paper and a pen or pencil, then list the pluses and minuses of the man's performance as they know it, and come to some consensus as to what the manager's strengths and weaknesses are.

The purposes back of group appraisals are to reduce the immediate superior's bias, to bring in factors of performance that he would probably not have known, or to call to his attention appraisal information he might have forgotten. It has much to commend it. However, there are many drawbacks to group appraisal. One is the danger involved in peer appraisals noted above. Another is the time required for the process. Still another is the difficulty of getting a suitable group of people who really know a manager's work, although this can be helped by asking the person to be rated to nominate a panel of people who are likely to know his work and selecting from it.

Further difficulties are those encountered with all committee operations: the problem of getting a meaningful consensus without undue compromise and the failure of groups to feel individual responsibility. Still another weakness is that the group appraisal, if held confidential, may be looked upon as a "star chamber" proceeding. If the considerations and discussion of the group leak out, the whole appraisal proceeding might well miss the objective and constructive purposes so central to effective evaluation.

Ranking   One of the fairly widely used methods of forcing discrimination in evaluation is to require the rater to list his subordinates on each factor, rated in rank order from the best to the least able. By arranging individuals in order of merit, certain advantages result. It is a simple process, at least in doing so by each characteristic being rated. Also, it is a kind of thing that even managers without much experience in or knowledge of evaluation can do.

Yet ranking has the disadvantage of providing nothing more than an ordered listing of individuals in a particular group. This method yields no real insights into the nature or the magnitude of differences within the group. The results are also of little diagnostic value and do not suggest areas of concentration for an individual to improve in order to get a better ranking. Accordingly, they are not very useful as motivators since they offer no definite way in which an undesirable situation can be improved.

In addition, the task of ranking increases in difficulty as the number of people being rated increases. Furthermore, the rankings in various groups cannot be compared with each other. It is entirely possible that a man ranked seventh in one group might be better than the top-ranked man in another.

In case groups are fairly large, rank ordering can be helped by the *paired comparison* method. This involves systematic comparison of each individual within a group. Each person being rated is compared with every other man, and the final ranking of a person is determined by the number of times he was judged better than the others. While this device does help in ranking, it can be seen that with any fairly large group the number of paired comparisons can be quite large. Thus, with ten persons to be ranked, the number of judgments, given by the formula $\frac{n(n-1)}{2}$, would be 45, and if rankings for ten persons are made on each of twelve traits or qualities, the number of judgments required would jump to some 7,140.

While ranking has deficiencies and difficulties, its use as an offset to the nondiscriminating ratings often made can be helpful. As a means for an individual to see the weakness of his appraisals and learn the practical meaning of "average," it has much to commend it. But as a method of appraisal for general application, it can hardly be recommended very strongly.

Forced Choice   In order to reduce bias, one of the better systems of rating is a forced-choice type of questionnaire. In this method, originally developed by the U.S. Army for officer evaluation, a number of statements or adjectives—usually four to a set—are developed from experience and tests, to reflect some phase of a manager's characteristics or job. Two of the statements or adjectives are indicative of poor managing and two of good managing. The rater is then required to select which of the four is most characteristic of the person rated and which is least.

Some examples from the original Army officer efficiency report that illustrate the rating against which the rater is required to select the *one* that is most applicable to the person and the one that is least characteristic are:

With respect to job proficiency:
1. Becomes dogmatic about authority.
2. Careless and slipshod in attention to duty.
3. No one ever doubts his ability.
4. Well-grounded in all phases of Army life.

or

1. Follows closely directions of higher echelons.
2. Inclined to "goldbrick."
3. Criticizes unnecessarily.
4. Willing to accept responsibility.

or

1. Fails to support fellow officers.
2. Oversteps his authority.
3. Gives clear and concise direction.
4. Very exacting in all details.

Likewise a prominent company developed such tetrads as the following:

1. Insists upon his subordinates being precise and exact.
2. Allows himself to be burdened with detail.
3. Stimulates associates to be interested in their work.
4. Does not point out when work is poorly done.

or

1. His subordinates like him.
2. Does not delegate.

3. Is very decisive.
4. Has great technical knowledge.

In a typical forced-choice appraisal system there may be a number of these tetrads. In the original U.S. Army system, for example, there were twelve on job proficiency and twelve on personal qualifications. The most and least characteristic ones in each tetrad were correlated from empirical data and case experience with success factors of officers actually in service. Since the rater does not know what these correlations are and is forced to make a choice, it was believed that the element of bias could thereby be removed. This belief was buttressed by experimentation in applying the system to officers whose reputation as outstanding, average, or poor was well known from other measures.

Particularly if an appraisal system is based on traits or work characteristics, the forced-choice method has a great deal of merit. But to be truly meaningful, different tests would have to be devised for various positions in a company. The work of doing so and validating the tests empirically would seem to be overwhelming. At the same time, there are probably enough similarities in the basics of managing so that a standard system could have general utility in appraising managers as managers. Even were this attempted, the task of validation would appear to be extremely difficult.

Moreover, because the validity of forced-choice measurement depends upon keeping fairly secret the method of scoring, to avoid "beating the system," the feedback advantage for constructive management development is lacking. Also, raters tend to resist participating in an evaluation system where they do not know the ratings they are giving. On the other hand there are companies which have professed success with the system.

Critical Incident Method   Another device for giving meaning to trait and performance characteristic evaluation has been the use of critical incidents. In its essentials, this technique operates by superiors collecting instances of their subordinates performing in ways that, through prior analysis, have been shown to be of critical importance to the success or failure of the job being appraised.

In what is perhaps the original program, aimed only at hourly employees, some 2,500 critical incidents describing specific deeds that represented either good or detrimental behavior were collected.[6] These incidents were then further analyzed and grouped into sixteen critical job requirements under the categories of physical and mental qualifications and work habits and attitudes. All the subheadings under these two categories were traits or performance characteristics, such as "coordination," "showing inventiveness," "productivity," "dependability," "getting along with others," and "responsibility." Under each of these categories, sample critical incident behaviors were listed.

The rater was then encouraged to keep a record of critical incidents and periodically enter them under the proper category as good or poor behavior examples. The supervisor then used these as a subject of review with the worker and as a source for performance improvement.

Strictly speaking, the incident approach is not a real rating system although, if enough incidents could be accumulated, it could have great benefit when a manager came to rate his subordinate. Nor is there evidence that the system has been used widely for managerial, in contrast to hourly employee, appraisal. It is included here mainly because many managers

[6] As reported in J. C. Flanagan and R. K. Burns, "The Employee Performance Record: A New Appraisal and Development Tool," *Harvard Business Review*, vol. 33, no. 5, pp. 95–102 (September–October, 1955).

and others interested in evaluation have raised questions from time to time about its possible applicability.

The system does have merit. However, it is difficult to form a good initial classification of incidents. Experience has also proved that supervisors, even when pressure is applied, do not keep adequate records of critical incidents. As a supplement to the better appraisal systems discussed in succeeding chapters, however, the approach might be given consideration.

chapter three

Appraisal against
Verifiable Objectives:
Nature

One of the most exciting tools that has swept across the managerial scene in the past decade is the system of appraising managerial performance against accomplishment of preselected verifiable objectives. As noted in the opening chapter, setting a network of meaningful and actionable objectives lies at the base of all managing. This is a simple logic, since no one can be expected to accomplish a task with effectiveness or efficiency unless he knows what the end point of his efforts should be. Nor can any organized enterprise in business or elsewhere be expected to do so.

Yet it is one of the strange phenomena of human history that only in fairly recent years have an increasing number of those responsible for managing our various organizations come to realize that, if objectives are to be actionable, they must be clear and verifiable to those who pursue them. No one can accomplish an ambiguous goal. He must know what his goals are, which actions contribute to their attainment, and when they have been accomplished. As basic as utilizing verifiable objectives is, it is nonetheless difficult in practice. As simple as the concept is, too few businesses are really so managing and it is only an exceedingly rare nonbusiness operation that is even attempting to do so.

Origins of the Objectives Approach

It is not strictly accurate to pick out anyone who originated the approach emphasizing objectives because common sense has told people for many centuries that groups and individuals expect to accomplish some end results. However, there have been certain individuals who have long placed emphasis on management by objectives and, by doing so, have given impetus to its development as a system.

One of these is Peter Drucker. In 1954, he acted as a catalyst by emphasizing that "objectives are needed in every area where performance and results directly and vitally affect the survival and prosperity of the business" and "the performance that is expected of the manager must be derived from the performance goals of the business, his results must be measured by the contribution they make to the success of the enterprise."[1] This in turn requires "management by objectives" and "control by self-control."

At the same time, if not indeed earlier than Drucker, the General Electric Company laid out the elements of managing

---

[1] *The Practice of Management* (New York: Harper & Brothers, 1954), pp. 63, 101.

by objectives in its extensive planning for reorganization in 1952-1954.[2] The company pointed out at that time that:

> Decentralization of managerial decision-making requires that objective goals and objective measurements of progress toward these goals be substituted for subjective appraisals and personal supervision. Through a program of objective measurements, managers will be equipped to focus attention on the relevant, the trends, and on the future. To the extent, therefore, that we are able to develop sound, objective measurements of business performance, our philosophy of decentralizing authority and responsibility will be rendered more effective [p. 113].

The company implemented this philosophy of appraisal by identifying key result areas and undertaking considerable research on their measurement. However, there is no evidence that it was actually placed in operation by a program of appraising performance against verifiable objectives as we know it today. Nonetheless, the report reflects a pioneering approach to the problem.

Likewise, too, in 1957, Douglas McGregor, in his classic paper criticizing trait appraisal systems as requiring "the manager to pass judgment on the personal worth of subordinates" and thereby "playing God," made a strong plea toward appraising on the basis of preset objectives.[3] McGregor's concern was with the then (and largely now) conventional appraisal methods which emphasized personal characteristics. He saw in appraisal against objectives a means of making evaluations constructive and placing the emphasis where it ought to be, on performance rather than on personality. Its main advantage, according to McGregor, would be to stimu-

[2] See especially *Professional Management in General Electric* (New York: The General Electric Company, 1954), Book Three, "The Work of the Professional Manager," pp. 24-28, 38-42, 113-132.

[3] "An Uneasy Look at Performance Appraisal," *Harvard Business Review*, vol. 35, no. 3, pp. 89-94 (May-June, 1957).

late development of subordinates and give them means for greater motivation.

Considerable push to the trend toward emphasizing objectives was also given by Edward Schleh's stimulating book on *Management by Results,* published in 1961.[4] He suggested that "management objectives state the specific accomplishment expected of each individual in a specific period of time so that the work of the whole management group is soundly blended at a particular moment of time" and that "objectives should be set for personnel all the way down to each foreman and salesman and, in addition, to staff people such as accountants, industrial engineers, chemists, etc."[5] Schleh recommended that delegation be by results expected and that appraisals be geared to the same standard.

Mentioning the basic contributions of Drucker, General Electric, McGregor, and Schleh may be unfair to their many predecessors and successors. Henri Fayol emphasized objectives, Lyndall Urwick built much of his management writing around accomplishment of objectives, and Chester Barnard made purpose the distinguishing feature of formal organizations—all their work, and much by so-called classicists, done many years before 1954. But the emphasis on actually *appraising* managers against their accomplishment of preset objectives largely developed in the late 1950's and even more particularly in the 1960's.

However, much of the early emphasis on management by objectives in the many books and articles published in the 1960's and much of the practice then and now has failed to refine the concept to require *verifiable* objectives. As long as objectives are stated in general terms, as was noted in the discussion of key result areas in the previous chapter, they

[4] Edward Schleh, *Management by Results,* (New York: McGraw-Hill Book Company, 1961).
[5] *Ibid.,* pp. 18–19.

can have little meaning for action and little for an objective appraisal of performance.

It is probably true that interest in developing a more objective and performance-oriented system of appraising managers gave major impetus to the modern growth of total management by objectives. As interest in appraisal shifted from personality to performance and the search for objectivity in appraisal grew, it was natural and normal that attempts should be made to develop more verifiable objectives.

The Nature of Management by Verifiable Objectives

As is eminently clear, a system of managing, or appraising managers by verifiable objectives, is a reflection of the purpose of managing itself. Without clear purpose, managing is haphazard and random, and no individual and no group can expect to perform effectively or efficiently unless a clear goal is sought. If, then, this is the purpose of managing, it follows that we should evaluate managers against this standard.

But there is more to it than this.

Quantitative Objectives It has been noted at various points that to be meaningful objectives must be verifiable. The easiest way to get verifiability is to put goals in quantitative terms. Instead of saying a goal is to make a profit, we must say that it is to make $10 million in profit after taxes in 1972 by selling $200 million of products—with $40 million in product line A, $60 million in product line B, $20 million in product line C, and $80 million in product line D—at a gross profit margin of 33 percent, a net profit before taxes of 10 percent, and a return on stockholders' equity of 18 percent.

For a manufacturing manager, his goals might be to produce two million items at a total direct cost of $100 million and period costs not to exceed $33 million, to reduce scrap from 2.5 percent to 2.0 percent, to keep factory labor turnover under 4 percent per month, or to purchase and install a given type of plant equipment at a cost not to exceed $3 million by December 15, 1972.

Similar quantitative goals could be made for other positions on down the line. Even a packaging line foreman in a given month might have goals to package 500 cases of product per hour, with a labor cost not to exceed 5 cents per case, and with a scrap factor not in excess of 1 percent. The district sales manager might have objectives of selling in his district 25,000 cases of merchandise in a month, with a sales volume of $250,000, and having his sales force make an average of six calls per man per day. Or a personnel manager might have a department goal to recruit 100 persons of various specific qualifications each month, to hold exit interviews with each departing employee within one day of his separation, and to reduce clerical costs in his department by 4 percent.

Qualitative Objectives   Unfortunately, many goals cannot be quantified. In fact, there is a danger in attempting to push numbers too far since the specious accuracy of numbers in many areas can lead managers astray. There is the danger that numbers and mathematics may even tend to replace managing. Moreover, there are too many worthwhile goals that are not quantitative, and the higher one goes in the management structure, the more objectives are likely to be qualitative.

Qualitative goals can, for the most part, be made verifiable, although admittedly not with the complete degree of accuracy possible in quantitatively stated objectives. For example, a training manager may have a goal to develop and implement a certain new program of training with certain specified characteristics by a certain date. Or a company controller may be charged with devising, with the cooperation of affected line managers, a program of variable budgeting, by a certain date, with expense variations spread over volumes of sales outputs from $350,000 to $650,000 per month. The manufacturing manager might have, as one of his objectives, the development and installation of a certain program of equipment realignment by a given date. Likewise, the head of research and development might have an objective of completing the design of a new product with certain specifications by a certain date.

Sometimes it is said that qualitative objectives are gauged by the standard of "how well" and quantitative objectives by "how much." To some extent this is true, but the author's experience is that any qualitative goal can be made highly verifiable by spelling out the characteristics of the program or other objective sought and a date of accomplishment. If it can be said, for example, that an objective is "to make more effective use of personnel recruitment services," it can almost as easily be said "to make more effective use of personnel recruitment services by (1) requiring all new positions below a certain level to be submitted to the personnel department; (2) having the personnel department develop a program (with certain specified characteristics) for publicizing its approaches and services within the company by June 30; and (3) having the personnel department develop and implement a program of regular follow-up on candidates recommended to line managers by May 1."

The essence of making qualitative objectives meaningful is preplanning approximately how these will be accomplished. While there still may be some judgment required as to "how well" a program or other qualitative objective is accomplished, if a completion date is specified, its accomplishment or failure can be substantiated. The more the basic characteristics are thought through, the more verifiable the goals.

This is as it should be. Objectives tend to be meaningless

if they represent an end point where no thinking as to how to get there has been done and to be equally empty if the "how well" has to cope with such generalities as "make more effective use," "improve," "increase," "simplify," or "speed up," without these terms being given some confirmable meaning.

Verifiability Is the Key   It should be abundantly clear at this point that verifiability is the key to useful objectives. Even though some subjective judgment of the "how well" type may have to be applied, it should be minimal. And it can be, with proper thought and planning.

The biggest problem is not usually "how well" but rather "how much" of a goal accomplishment is acceptable as good performance. This becomes especially difficult when unforeseen circumstances occur or the failure of performance at another place in the goal network thwarts an individual's accomplishment. The critical question to raise is whether these circumstances should have caused a "miss" and by "how much."

One of the interesting experiences the author has had is working with a government agency that has been installing a program of management by verifiable objectives. In this rare and admirable case, many of the department heads' objectives were qualitative. In asking these managers to come up with objectives, as a first step, it was not surprising to find many like the following:

Inform more people of available health services.

Use personnel methods designed to secure and retain high-caliber public employees.

Select and organize a staff in such a way as to best accomplish the departmental objective.

Eliminate all possible time now wasted in unproductive action.

Refine and manage the work program.

Establish an ongoing program for data processing personnel.

One must recognize that, particularly in some departments of typical government agencies, setting verifiable objectives is extremely difficult. Nevertheless, as each department manager was asked the simple question, "At the end of the year how will you know whether this objective has been accomplished?" or "How will your subordinates know when they are accomplishing an objective?" a little thought made it possible to develop highly verifiable objectives. For example, the general objective on health services became one "to increase the utilization of public health services during the fiscal year by 15 percent (as measured by the number of persons using the services) through specific programs of (1) developing three decentralized medical clinics; (2) establishing night clinics in two locations; and (3) geographically consolidating various preventive health services." Each program included enough specific characteristics and even quantitative data to make the objectives highly verifiable and meaningful to the department manager and his subordinates.

Budgetary Objectives and Other Objectives   It is sometimes argued that all a manager really needs is a well-planned and constructed budget and this will furnish all the objectives required. The argument is that, if a budget is based on sound planning premises, including especially a credible sales forecast, and an acceptable level of profit, all the department managers need to do is to meet the budget, item by item.

It is true that a good budget, like a clear and accurate profit and loss statement and balance sheet, is a summary, in numerical terms, of what a business plans. It is true, too, that any well-constructed financial summary can be a "window" through which the plans and activities of managers can be seen if the observer looks far enough.

But more is needed in practice. Budget figures are resultants of plans and expected performance. They have meaning only when backed by actionable plans and programs. The end points of each plan must be some goal toward which actions are aimed.

Thus a marketing department might have a goal to accomplish sales of $20 million in a given year. To do this, however, programs must be made for pinpointed market research, for developing sales promotions with certain characteristics by a certain time, for launching advertising programs with certain features during a given period, and for specific deployment and preparation of the field sales force. In each of these areas, too, the organizational subcomponents should have plans and objectives to contribute toward the accomplishment of the various programs. In addition, the marketing area plans and objectives normally need to be supported by coordinate supporting programs in such areas as new product development, purchasing, production, shipping, warehousing, costing, and pricing.

Without a workable network of plans and objectives, budget figures themselves tend to be wishes or guesses. Yet no one would exclude from a set of objectives the meeting of budget commitments.

How Management by Objectives Works

Although the interest in this book in management by objectives is as a means of managerial appraisal, it should be pointed out again that it is really a system of managing. Appraising performance against verifiable objectives is not a separate exercise from managing. It is an integral part of doing the managerial job.

Can Start at Any Level   The ideal system is one in which setting of varifiable objectives starts at the top of the enterprise, has the active support of the chief executive, and goals are even set for him. That this can be done is illustrated by the set of objectives a chief executive of a medium-sized company developed with the assistance of a small committee of the board of directors. These are outlined in Table 3.

TABLE 3   Verifiable Goals of Company President for Year, 1971

I. *Sales and Profit Goals — 1971:*

Operating division	1971 sales	Increase over 1970, %	Pretax profit as percent of sales	Profit before taxes	Pretax profit as return on investment, %
Test equipment	$ 9,500,000	12.0	12.0	$1,140,000	24.0
Engineering test facilities	2,400,000	15.0	10.0	240,000	42.0
Medical equipment	6,700,000	22.0	16.2	1,085,400	34.0
Control instruments	12,300,000	20.0	13.6	1,672,800	30.0
Electronic components	5,100,000	24.0	14.8	754,800	40.0
	$36,000,000	18.3	13.6	$4,893,000	30.6

II. *An improved system of profit planning* in effect throughout the company by September 30, 1971, with the following characteristics:
   1. A system of variable budgets for the company as a whole, for each division, and each department designed to reach the sales and profit goals of the company and divisions.
   2. A program of sales forecasts made one year in advance and revised quarterly.
   3. A program of regular (not less than semiannual) review of variable budget bases.
   4. An actual monthly, twelve-month moving average, and year-to-date summary report of performance against budgets.

III. *An improved new product development program* for each major product area of the company, designed to assure an increase in company sales of 20 percent per year, to be in effect by June 30, 1971, with the following major features:

1. Review and selection of new products and product improvements which will be consistent with the company's financial resources, maintenance of profit levels, its engineering and production capabilities, and its marketing abilities.
2. *Submission of major new product or product improvement programs* involving an expenditure of more than $20,000 in engineering, production facilities, and market test and promotion to the board of directors for approval.
3. *Programming of product development projects* which will assure completion within budgeted time and costs.
4. *Control of information flow* which will give adequate information on the progress of product development projects.
5. *Formal, rigorous, and regular review of new product and product improvement selection and progress.*
6. *Monthly summary reports* of all new product and product improvements selected, of program, and progress to the board of directors.

IV. *A revised chart of executive approval authorizations,* to be submitted to the board of directors by March 31, 1971 and regularly (not less often than semiannually) reviewed with a view to revision thereafter.

V. *An organization plan* for three to five years in advance to be submitted to the board by September 30, 1971, based on, among other things:

1. A recognition of the importance of profit responsibility by individual managers.
2. The availability and capacities of present managerial personnel.
3. The needs for training of present management personnel.
4. The requirements for recruitment of new managerial personnel.
5. The necessity of considering proper centralization of authority at top corporate levels and the need for appropriate decentralized authority to division and functional managers.
6. Consideration of the costs and advantages of divisional product, or other decentralized functional departmentation.

VI. *A proposed program of compensation of key managerial personnel,* including salary adjustments, the initiation of bonuses and stock options, and adequate fringe benefits, to be submitted to the board by September 30, 1971.

VII. *A program of new plant facilities* for the medical equipment and control instruments divisions, including the gradual move to such facilities, to be submitted to the board by June 30, 1971, which will:

1. Not materially reduce profit in the current operating years when moves must take place.

TABLE 3   (cont.)

    2. Improve earnings of the company in the near future (i.e., within two years).

    3. Provide for minimum losses on present lease obligations.

    4. Provide for minimum possible losses of trained personnel.

VIII. *An acquisition program,* to be submitted to the board by July 15, 1971, based on the following principles:

    1. The acquisition must fit the company's capabilities in marketing, engineering, and manufacturing, or must bring such capabilities into the company.

    2. It must be within the company's financial capabilities.

    3. It must improve the company's earning position:

        a. It must provide, at least after integration, for a return on net assets and net worth above that now being made.

        b. It must increase the earnings per share of company stock after the acquisition.

    4. Normally, the acquisition must include an element of effective management, or the company must see the ability to acquire effective management for it.

This set of goals might be regarded by some as too extensive, but it should not be forgotten that the president himself will not do all these things. Through delegation and effective control he will see that they are done. Also, it will be noted that many of the objectives are qualitative but all are reasonably verifiable, even though there will still be some room for judging how well they will be done. In addition, it can be seen that these goals establish a framework from which the division manager and others down the line can aim their own objectives.

While it is best that objective setting start at the top, it is not necessary that it do so. It can start at a division level, at a marketing manager level, or even lower. This has happened. In one company the author worked with over ten years ago, the system started in one division where it was carried down to first-level supervision in an interlocking network within the division. Under the personal leadership and tutelage of the division general manager, it succeeded in profitability, cost reduction, and improved operations. Soon, some other division managers and the chief executive became interested in, and attempted to implement, similar programs.

The author has even seen cases where the start was made at a middle-management level. The head of an accounting section started in one case and his success not only gave him recognition (and promotion) but served as an entrance point for the entire company to embark on a program.

The Critical Importance of Planning Premises   No one can be expected to set meaningful objectives without some premises, or assumptions, of the future. These may be external influences such as expected price levels, gross national product, population changes, or supply costs and availability. Or they may be internal factors such as the status of new product development, major company policies, the availability of cash and other resources, or labor union contracts in effect.

The important point is that, since plans necessarily operate in the future, he who would plan meaningfully must have a clear idea of what kind of future his plans must fit. Even though there are uncertainties, no manager can plan—set objectives and means of reaching them—without some idea of the kind of future in which his plans will probably operate. It is the stage on which planned action will take place. While it is obviously impractical to sketch out this future in too much detail, the critical factors of most importance to an operation can and must be premised. Without it, goals are guesses or wishes and plans are random hopes.

This is even more important to subordinate managers. They cannot be asked to establish goals, plans, or budgets without critical guidelines or premises. No one can plan for a vacuous future, and those who are asked to do so without guidelines will consciously or unconsciously devise their own. These, of course, may or may not fit company thinking and expectations. In this event, also, only by sheer accident will the goals

Chart I

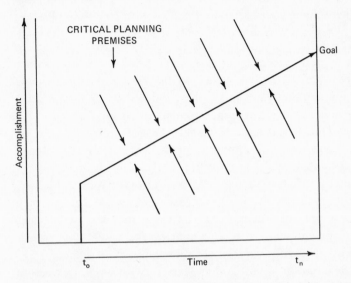

CRITICAL PLANNING
PREMISES

Goal

Accomplishment

t_o Time t_n

Plans operate in the future and there are always critical future events (premises) that affect the course of programs.

and plans of one manager fit those of others, since each person's premises are likely to vary in important respects.

Preliminary Setting of Objectives at the Top   Given appropriate planning premises, the first step in setting objectives is for the top manager concerned to determine what he perceives to be the more important goals he wants his company to achieve in a given period ahead. These can be set for any period—a quarter, a year, or for five years—whatever is felt desirable in given circumstances. In most instances they are set to coincide with the annual budget. But this is not necessary and often not desirable. Certain goals should be scheduled for accomplishment in a much shorter period and others for a much longer period. Also, particularly as one goes down the line in an organization, goal accomplishment of managers tends to have a shorter time span. It is seldom feasible or wise for a first-line supervisor, for example, to set many annual goals, since his goal span on most operating matters, such as cost or scrap reduction, rearrangement of facilities, or instituting of special personnel programs, is short and may be measured in weeks or months.

The goals first set by the top manager must be looked upon as being preliminary, based on his analysis and judgment of what can and should be accomplished by his organization in a period of time, and taking into account its strengths and weaknesses, in the light of opportunities facing him. They must be regarded as tentative and subject to modification as the entire chain of verifiable objectives is worked out by his organization. It is foolish to push top-management-dictated objectives down the throats of subordinates, since forced objectives can hardly induce an indispensable sense of subordinate commitment. Most managers also find in the process of working out goals with subordinates both problems to be dealt with and opportunities they could not have previously known.

In the setting of objectives, the manager also establishes measures of what will indicate goal accomplishment. If verifiable objectives are developed, these measures, whether in dollars of sales or profits, percentages, cost levels, or program execution will normally be built into the objectives.

Clarification of the Organizational Roles   Often overlooked in installing and operating programs of management by objectives is the relationship between results expected and the location of responsibility to attain them. Ideally, every goal and subgoal should be some one person's clear responsibility. Analysis of the organization structure in terms of results expected will often show areas of fuzziness where clarification or reorganization is called for. Sometimes it is impossible to mold an organization so that a given objective is some one person's or organization unit's responsibility. In setting goals for launching a new product, for example, careful coordination will normally be required of the managers of research, marketing, and production. These separate responsibilities can be largely centralized by putting a product manager in charge. But if this is not desirable, at least the specific parts of each coordinating manager's contribution to the total program goal can and should be clearly identified.

Setting of Subordinates' Objectives After making sure that pertinent general objectives, strategies, and planning premises are disseminated to the subordinate manager concerned, the superior can then proceed to work with him in setting his objectives. The superior will normally give his subordinate his *preliminary* thinking on the goals he has believed feasible for the company or department he manages. At this point, and preferably before he meets with his subordinate, the superior will ask what goals the subordinate believes he can accomplish, in what time period, and with what resources.

The superior's role at this point is extremely important. He must take the position: "What can you do?" "How can we improve your operation to help me improve mine?" "What stands in the way, what obstructions keep you from a higher level of performance?" "What changes can we make?" "How can I help?" It is amazing how many things can be found that obstruct performance and can be removed, and how many diamonds of constructive ideas can be dredged from the experience and knowledge of subordinates.

The superior must also be a patient counselor, helping his subordinate to develop consistent and supportive objectives and watching to see that he does not set goals impossible or highly improbable of attainment. Human nature tends to be the same. Anything can be accomplished a year hence, but much less by tomorrow. And one of the things that can kill a program of managing by objectives is to allow managers to set up "blue sky" objectives that they cannot reasonably be expected to accomplish.

At the same time, goal setting by subordinates does not

represent the same principles as "progressive education"—where people do whatever they want to do. The superior must listen and work with his subordinate, but, in the end, he must take responsibility for approving his subordinate's goals. His judgment and final approval must be based upon what is reasonably attainable with "stretch" and "pull," what is fully supportive of upper-level objectives, what is consistent with goals of other managers in other functions, and what goals will not be inconsistent with the longer-run objectives and interests of the department and company.

Advantages in a Group Approach to Goal Setting Although not necessary, the author has found great advantages in having a committee, or group, participate in goal-setting sessions. Immediate superiors tend to have an almost paternalistic interest in their subordinates and can be overly sympathetic with their problems and limitations. The ideal method is to have an appropriate committee (not the kind of group discussed on pp. 37–38) review both performance and objectives at each level. A division general manager is now usually reviewed by a company executive or administrative committee, made up of headquarters functional staff executives and chaired by the president (even though it should never be forgotten by other committee members that the division manager is the subordinate of the president).

If this standard practice is good for division general managers, it has merit for their subordinates. A plant manager might be reviewed by a committee made up of the division manager, the manufacturing director (the plant manager's superior), an industrial or plant engineer on the manufacturing manager's staff, or perhaps the director of materiel or the chief engineer. A foreman might be reviewed by a group consisting of his immediate superior—the plant superintendent, plus the plant manager—the superintendent's superior, and an industrial engineer.

It will be noted that the committees that have been suggested to review a manager's performance and goals consist of the immediate superior, the superior's superior, and one or more staff specialists. The purposes of suggesting this are several. In the first place, a group to review and help a person set goals gives the whole proceeding a formality and rigor not usually possible with only an immediate superior. It is true that many managers being reviewed by such a group refer to the system as the "sweatbox," but they almost universally like it. They are forced to do a more thorough job of thinking their problems and objectives out in advance. It also has the advantage of having persons who are technically more able to ask questions, probe problems, dig into gaps in preparation and performance.

In addition, by having the immediate superior's superior involved, a number of benefits can result: the immediate superior becomes less of a "filter" for problems and constructive suggestions; a degree of management support not otherwise possible is given the process; a chance to appraise the quality of his immediate subordinate and his subordinates is given the superior's superior; and the latter represents an additional echelon of authority to make most decisions in problem areas on the spot, or, at least, he has the additional stature to get problems more readily resolved by higher authority.

The author has had the opportunity to sit in on some of these committee review sessions. In one first-level review, a packaging line supervisor was being reviewed. His objectives were fairly simple: number of cases per hour, scrap factor in percent, direct labor hours required, improvements in working conditions. In the course of the discussion, one of the reviewers asked him whether he knew of any way to improve the output of the packaging line without tearing down the factory and starting over again. The supervisor immediately responded that he could increase output by 25 percent with the same labor hours. When asked how he would do that, the supervisor pointed out some modifications he would make to the line. When asked if he knew how much such a change would cost, he readily responded, "$18,000." Whereupon the plant manager turned to the industrial engineer and asked him whether such a change was feasible, to which the engineer replied that he thought so.

At this point the plant manager, who did not have corporate authority to approve such an $18,000 expenditure but knew he would have no trouble in getting his superiors to approve it for such a sizeable increase in efficiency, said, "We will study this suggestion this afternoon and if it turns out the way it looks, it is approved as of now!" One could see the first-level supervisor glow with pride and could imagine him telling his wife that evening that "I told them how to run the company today!" Also, one knew that, since this was his suggestion and he had obviously given it considerable study and thought, he would *make* it work.

An interesting sequel to this case came later in the meeting when the plant manager said: "Bill, that line change was a great idea. Why didn't you suggest it before?" To this question, the supervisor retorted: "I did a year ago and nothing happened; so I decided if that is the way you guys want to run this company, the hell with it!"

The use of a structure of committees to review performance and goals appears to be a time-consuming complex process. It does take time and effort. But it is worth it. As the head of a company told the author: "It took a lot of time, but do you know that since I have gotten this under way, for the first time since I have been president, I now have time to think." In other words, what he found out was that he and his subordinates, by spending their time in this way and answering questions, getting agreement on objectives and actions, and making decisions to clear the way for future performance, did not have to go through the more time-consuming and wearisome task of dealing with countless piecemeal problems, managerial fire fighting, and detailed control of people who were missing plans they did not understand or could not accomplish.

Goals and Resources   One of the major advantages of setting up a careful network of verifiable goals and a requirement for doing so effectively is to tie in the need for capital, material, and human resources at the same time. Any manager at any level requires these resources to accomplish his goals. By relating these to the goals themselves, superiors are better able to see the need and economics of allocating them. It helps to avoid the bane of any upper-level manager's existence—the "nickel and diming" by subordinates who need "one more technician or engineer" or "one more piece of equipment," which, in isolation, is easy for him to sell to his boss and difficult for the superior to refuse.

Recycling Objectives   As indicated, setting objectives can hardly be done by starting at the top and dividing them up. Nor should they be started from the bottom. What is required is a degree of recycling. The top manager may have an idea as to what his subordinates should set as objectives, and those who report to him for their subordinates, but the process of goal setting as outlined above will almost certainly change these preconceived goals as the contributions of subordinates come into focus. Thus, objectives setting is not only a joint process but also one of interaction which will require recycling.

This process is worth the time. People involved will have a better understanding of their targets and how they fit, they cannot help but have a better feeling of commitment to meet them, the structure of objectives is likely to be characterized by a better fit, and the people involved are more likely to meet them.

How Many Objectives?   Much discussion has occurred on the question of how many objectives an individual manager should have before him at a given time. Edward Schleh has stated that "no position should have more than two to five objectives" at one time.[6] His argument is that too many objectives tend to take the concentrated drive out of a program and to highlight minor objectives to the detriment of the major ones.

There is something to what Schleh says, but his number seems too arbitrary and too few. It is true that minor routine objectives should seldom be a part of a program unless we are dealing with a low-level, fairly routine job. Even in this case, there should be some objectives that are not a routine part of the job. It would not appear to be fruitful, for example, to include in a supervisor's plan the preparation of work assignments daily (unless it were something new and unusual) or the initialling of time reports and the reviewing of inspection reports. Nor would it be significant for an upper-level manager to have special objectives of meeting callers, attending meetings, or interviewing candidates for new positions. There are certain things which any manager is expected to do, and these need not be made into specific and special objectives. Objectives, as dealt with here, are not designed to deal with every facet of an individual's job. They should not be confused with activities.

But even if we exclude routine matters, it seems that there is not any specific number of objectives that should be the limit. To be sure, if there are so many that none stands out or commands attention, a program will fail. At the same time, it does seem possible that a manager might pursue in a normal period of time as many as ten or fifteen significant ob-

[6] Schleh, *op. cit.*, p. 22.

jectives. This depends in turn on how much he does himself and how much he can delegate, thereby limiting his role to one of assignment, supervising, and controlling. The important thing is that the objectives must be significant and critical to the total of a manager's performance.

Weighting Objectives   As may be seen from the sample of the chief executive's annual goals noted above and the samples of verifiable objectives shown in Table 4, not all are of the same importance. It is probably true that if the president made his sales and profit goals and missed many of the rest, he would probably not be in much trouble with his board of directors. And so it is the same with any manager's set of objectives.

While there is a tendency to resist weighting verifiable goals mainly because weightings are almost unavoidably subjective, there are many advantages in doing so, since clearly the missing or attainment of one objective may be far more or less important than another. This point was dramatized in a certain company where a division manager reported that one of his key subordinates had met 90 percent of his goals while another, whom he appraised lower, had met only 60 percent of his. A review of the two records showed that the highly rated man had missed key goals of profitability and new product introduction and marketing, against which his successes in other goals seemed to pale in significance. The lower-rated manager, on the other hand, had met his key objectives and had missed a number which, while important, did not rate in total with those he had accomplished.

As difficult as it may be and as subjective as it almost surely must be, there seems to be no alternative to giving some weighting to goals. This has the advantage of establishing priorities and helping superior managers make a better appraisal of performance.

Management by Objectives for Staff Positions

It is sometimes believed that meaningful objectives can only be established for line positions, since managers in these have direct responsibility for some phase of operating results. If we look at a staff position, as we should, as one where responsibility is to advise and counsel line managers with operating responsibilities, the question may be asked whether objectives can be set for these positions, since the staff man's primary job is help a person in a line position and make him succeed in his job.

Nevertheless, the author believes that objectives can be set for any position in an enterprise. As a matter of fact, in some cases this has been done. In the Radio Corporation of America, for instance, an active program has been applied to staff personnel for a decade.[7] While most staff objectives in this company could not be placed in quantitative terms, staff projects (even though advisory) were established in qualitative terms, indicating characteristics and target completion dates. Many involved "developing a method" or "conducting a study," or "finding the cause of" some problem. Thus most staff objectives, while verifiable, were qualitative.

The experience at RCA showed that some staff men even stated many quantitative objectives, such as "In 1964, I will save the company $—— through evaluation of new materials" or "Develop a cost reduction program that will reduce plant operating expenses by $—— ." To be sure, none of these staff individuals had the authority to implement any of these programs. They did, however, take the position that they had failed to meet an objective if the program they recommended

---

[7] As reported in W. S. Wikstrom, "Setting Targets for Staff," *The Conference Board Record,* vol. 1, no. 10, pp. 32–34 (October, 1964).

to operating managers was not good enough to be supported
and adopted and did not result in targeted savings.

An objective approach to staff work is important. It should
not be forgotten that the traditional definitional differentia-
tion between line—as those people contributing directly to
the attainment of enterprise objectives—and staff—as other
people who help the line—has unfortunate overtones. People
in a company should not be divided between those who accomplish objectives and others. Certainly no company interested in efficiency and effectiveness should tolerate anyone
on its payroll who does not contribute to attainment of enterprise objectives. Developing an ongoing program of staff work
by verifiable objectives is a step in the direction of making
clear what staff people can and should do.

Examples from Practice

While many books and articles have been written on management by objectives, rather few examples of actual practice
are available in the literature for the many enterprises who
have talked of management by objectives and who are thinking of undertaking it. Perhaps a few examples from several
positions in a real, but unnamed, company would be illumi-
nating. These are shown in Table 4. Others may be found in
Appendix One, where accomplishment is also shown.

Appraising Managers against
Verifiable Objectives

Once a program of managing by verifiable objectives is operating, appraisal is a fairly easy step. What is involved is seeing
how well a manager has performed against these preset objectives. This can be seen outlined in Charts II and III which

TABLE 4   Selected Examples of Verifiable Objectives

GENERAL MANAGER (DOMESTIC DIVISION)

A. *Sales and Profits by Product Line for Year*

	Sales in 000's	Gross profit in 000's	Gross profit percentage to sales
Product A	$ 934	$ 224	24.0
Product B	977	371	38.0
Product C	7,171	1,800	25.1
Product D	1,505	701	46.6
Product E	2,537	1,051	44.6
New Products	2,421	758	31.3
Total	$15,545	$4,905	31.6

B. *Burden and Period Expenses*

	Amount in 000's	Percent to net sales
Mfg. Burden	$ 717	4.6
Material	369	2.4
Marketing	642	4.1
Engineering	120	.8
Research & Development	95	.6
General and Administrative	244	1.6
Total Divisional Expenses	$2,187	14.1
Divisional Operating Profit	$2,718	17.5

C. *Secure an Operations Manager* by April 30, 1970 who will take responsibility for all operating areas except marketing and research and development and who can be a suitable second-in-command for the General Manager.

D. *Develop an acceptable and workable variable budget* by June 30, 1970 which will make possible an increase of sales (except for new products) above plan by 10 percent without an increase in period expenses.

E. *Develop a new marketing program* for product C by April 30, 1970 with the following characteristics:
   1. Designed to meet competition in the Eastern states by adding fifteen new distributors.
   2. Designed to promote user acceptance of the product by increasing direct mail contact with and service demonstrations for 5,400 users in the states of New York, Massachusetts, New Jersey, and Pennsylvania.
   3. Provide advertising support of $75,000 for forty-five distributors in the Eastern states.

TABLE 4 (cont.)

PLANT MANAGER (PLANT TWO)

A. Achieve production goals of product C with forty-six direct labor personnel assigned to the department by December 31, 1970.
B. Achieve production goals with two eight-hour shifts and not more than 5 percent of total direct labor costs in overtime pay by September 30, 1970.
C. Reduce industrial injuries and lost time days by 20 percent by December 31, 1970.
D. Undertake complete rework of production line A in accordance with approved program by June 1, 1970.
E. Reduce rework of product B by 400 units per week by September 30, 1970.

ADVERTISING MANAGER (DOMESTIC DIVISION)

A. *Expense Goals for 1970*

	Amount	Percent to sales
General and Administrative	$ 81,132	0.36
Print Shop	50,716	0.23
Advertising		
Products A, B, and C	270,000	2.9
Product D	45,600	3.0
Product E	83,800	3.3
New Products	146,500	3.5

B. *Develop and implement program* of corporate identity standardization:
  1. By designing and obtaining executive approval of new logo concept by March 31, 1970.
  2. By producing manual and instructions for integrating logo and formats in all domestic and international divisions by April 30, 1970.
  3. By implementing logo and format into all stationery by June 30, 1970 and into all packaging and advertising literature by September 30, 1970.

the St. Regis Paper Company has used to show "how" such appraisals are done and "why" they are done.

In those cases where appraisal by results has failed or been disillusioning, the cause has usually been traced to the fact that it was seen *only* as an appraisal tool. Even though search

Chart II
MANAGING FOR RESULTS: HOW IT IS DONE
                    St. Regis Paper Company

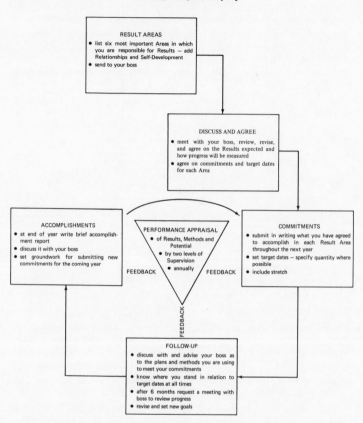

From W. S. Wikstrom, *Managing by—and with—Objectives* (New York: National Industrial Conference Board, Inc., 1968), p. 40.

for a better appraisal method probably gave managing by objectives its strongest impetus, it is likewise true that the system is not likely to work if only used as a means of appraisal. Management by objectives must be a way of man-

Chart III
MANAGING FOR RESULTS: WHY IT IS DONE
St. Regis Paper Company

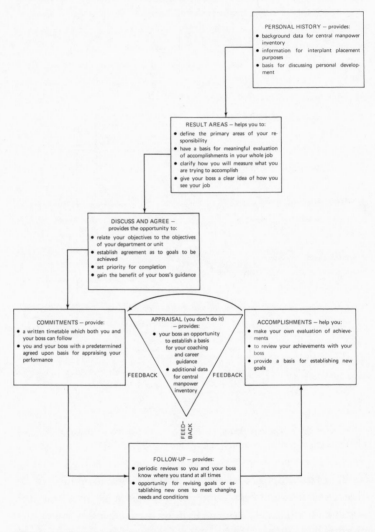

From W. S. Wikstrom, *Managing by—and with—Objectives* (New York: National Industrial Conference Board, Inc., 1968), p. 41.

aging, a way of planning, as well as the key to organizing, staffing, directing, and controlling. When it is this, then appraisal can be relatively easy. It boils down to: Did the manager establish adequate but reasonably attainable verifiable objectives, and how did he perform against them in a certain period?

But there are problems. Were the goals adequate? Did they call for "stretched" performance? These questions can only be answered by the judgment and experience of a man's superior, although this judgment can become sharper with experience and can take on a high degree of objectivity in those instances where goals of other managers in a similar position can be used for comparison. Did the manager actually establish verifiable objectives? Verifiability can be fairly easily determined and should be assured in the original goal-setting process. Were the objectives reasonably attainable? What were the intervening factors that kept a man from accomplishing his goals? Or what were the factors beyond his control that made accomplishment easy? And how should these be evaluated? Data on the reasons for failures or successes can and should be gathered. Nevertheless, since plans operate in the future and the future is always fraught with uncertainties, it is difficult for the reviewing officer to judge objectively and accurately reasons for nonaccomplishment or accomplishment.

Another problem that a reviewer must ever be watching is whether an individual keeps operating on obsolete goals when his situation has changed and revised goals should be established. In one company during the early years of its objectives program, a division manager explained his missing of profit and other goals by the costs and confusion of moving into a new and enlarged plant during the middle of the goal year. Of course, had he been alert, he would have foreseen this contingency and included its effect in his quarterly and annual goals. Or, at the very least, he should have submitted a new set of goals at midyear when he found the start-up problems to be greater than he could have anticipated.

Use of Summary Forms　To make a program of appraisal manageable, it is important for each superior to have a summary of goals in a form in which he can easily keep in mind what those of each subordinate are and can readily trace progress toward accomplishment. The form shown in Chart IV was found useful for division general managers in one company.

Regular Periodic Review　Progress toward goals should be regularly reviewed. For a top manager, such as a president or a division general manager, this progress should probably be reviewed quarterly in fair detail and more broadly for three or four additional quarters in the future. Goals can, and reasonably should, be tied to the annual budget, but experience has shown that only to set goals, or review them, annually is not enough. Alert and intelligent managers hardly wish to risk obsolete objectives, naturally prefer to have goal setting and evaluation a regular activity, and certainly in most instances would not wait an entire year to find out whether their subordinates have achieved their objectives. For dynamic management, annual reviews are just not enough.

For individuals below the top level, quarterly reviews may be frequent enough. And they may not. The real determinant is the time span necessary to ascertain whether a goal is still valid and whether progress is being made. It is probable for certain positions, such as those of first-level supervision, that reviews should usefully be made each month.

In appraising, too, the effective manager will give attention to priorities and weightings. As pointed out above, the number of goals, or the percentage of the total, accomplished or missed loses much of its significance if attention is not given to differences in importance.

What of Appraisal Forms?　If a superior manager has a complete and orderly picture of what his subordinates' objectives

Chart IV
SUMMARY OF PERFORMANCE AGAINST GOALS
FOR THE FOLLOWING:

NAME _____ TITLE _____ DIVISION _____

TYPES OF GOALS	GOALS Target Date	ACTUAL ACCOMPLISHMENT Date	ACTUAL ACCOMPLISHMENT Results	MANAGER'S OWN COMMENTS Date	SUPERIOR'S COMMENTS By ___ Date ___	SUPERIOR'S SUPERIOR'S COMMENTS By ___ Date ___
I. PROFITS & SALES						
a. Sales volume						
b. Gross profit						
c. Gross profit percentage						
d. Profit before royalties & taxes						
e. Other						
II. NEW PRODUCTS						
a. Product programs						
b. New product sales volume						
c. New product gross profit						
d. Other						
III. MARKETING						
a. Marketing programs						
b. Marketing expense						
c. Other						
IV. OPERATIONAL GOALS						
a. Basic operating expense variable budget						
b. Production expenses						
c. Operating expenses						
d. Gen'l & admin expense						
e. Inventories						
f. Receivables						
g. Other						
V. PLANT & FACILITIES						
a. Appropriation budgets						
b. Other						
VI. PERSONNEL POLICY & DEVELOPMENT						
a. Personnel report						
b. Labor turnover rate						
c. Other						

HOW TO USE

This form is an example only.

The types of goals (headings) on the left are designed for completion by each general manager on his performance against his goals. Bear in mind that the classification of goals under the main headings has not necessarily been completed. The headings include areas of types of goals which it would be expected that the GM would add and fill out those additional goal items which he feels he requires. The example of classifications on the left has purposely been condensed to be accommodated on this form, but actual tabulations should be spread out to utilize the space necessary.

As for persons other than general managers, it is suggested that the general manager create a list of areas appropriate for the goals of any given function manager and list them on blank forms.

were, and if he knows what the accomplishment record is, as he naturally should, no special appraisal form is necessary. However, for purposes of review by upper echelons of management and for personnel records for future reference, he might submit a summary statement of objectives set and performance against them. In addition, if the various objectives are given numerical weightings, these can be used in getting a rough summary rating of the overall performance.

Summary Ratings   It is often found useful, too, in addition to the weightings, to make estimates of percentage of completion of objectives. These, in turn, should be clarified, especially on missed goals, and even for materially exceeded objectives, by taking into account the nature and effect of extenuating or uncontrollable factors which led to the deviation. Setting percentage of completion or accomplishment in qualitative objectives introduces particularly subjective factors. There is some question as to how extensively they should be used for a summary rating for this reason.

Perhaps the best way to submit an evaluation of a manager's total performance against objectives is to submit the goal accomplishment form along with a narrative discussion and explanation of misses and successes. Having sat as a member of a board bonus committee of a company that uses these appraisals extensively, the author has found this kind of summary adequate and helpful for appraisal. After all, even with appraisal of performance against preset objectives, evaluation can hardly be mathematical.

Who Should Review Performance?   In addition to the immediate superior of the man being evaluated, it is recommended strongly that the superior's superior also make a review of the individual's performance and of the immediate superior's evaluation. As pointed out concerning evaluation in general earlier in this book, this has several advantages. Among these are the advantages of greater objectivity and a second look, the view that the superior's superior gets of his immediate subordinate's ability and his personnel, and the greater formality and weight given to the entire appraisal and management-by-objectives process.

There is even much to be said in having the same group that participated in the goal-setting session have a chance to participate in a review. As a matter of fact, this degree of formality and rigor in reviewing performance may be as important, in a constructive sense, it is hoped, as it is in setting objectives. Moreover, it has obvious advantages to the group and the person being reviewed to have this background in helping develop goals for a succeeding period.

Suggested Steps for Installing the Program

Perhaps there is no better way to summarize our discussion of the nature of managing by objectives and of a program of appraising performance against objectives than to highlight suggested steps for installing such a program. These may be seen graphically by referring to Chart V.

1. Teach the nature and philosophy of the program to all who will participate.

2. Establish and disseminate approved planning premises. These should include not only key assumptions of the external future the company or department expects to face, but also the strategies and policies expected to be controlling within.

3. Set preliminary objectives for the company or department by the top man concerned. At this stage, these need not be completely verifiable and can hardly be final, but should give clear direction to subordinates as to where it is hoped they will go.

4. Every superior, in considering his preliminary objectives, should determine what results he expects from each subordinate and assure himself that the organizational role and delegation of each is consistent with results expected.

Chart V
THE SYSTEM OF MANAGING AND APPRAISING BY OBJECTIVES

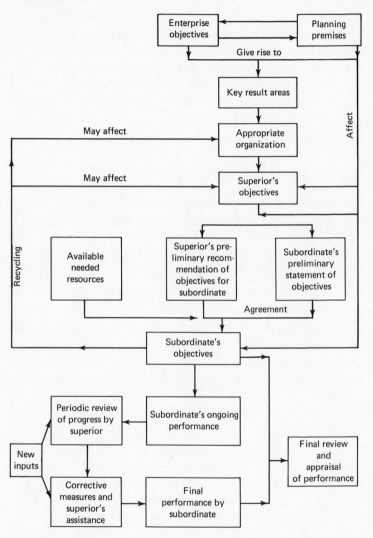

5. Ask each subordinate to set tentatively his own verifiable goals.

6. The superior then reviews his subordinate's goals with him. At this stage, the superior must ask and satisfy himself with the answers to the following questions:

 a. Are the goals verifiable?

 b. Are they supportive of the superior's goals?

 c. Are they consistent with planning premises?

 d. Are they consistent with and supportive to goals of other managers?

 e. Does the subordinate have the organizational authority and resources to accomplish the objectives? If not, can the superior furnish these?

 f. Do the objectives involve a reasonable amount of "stretch" and yet are they attainable?

 g. Can they be improved by any action the superior can take or get approved?

7. The superior approves his subordinate's goals.

8. If necessary, the superior sees that goals are reviewed and recycled up and down the line to make upper-level, as well as lower-level, goals consistent.

9. The superior periodically (at least quarterly and preferably oftener) reviews performance against goals, making suitable changes in goals or seeing that corrective action is taken to achieve desired performance.

10. The superior periodically appraises performance against goals, taking into account the quality of goals as well as performance.

chapter four

Appraisal against Verifiable Objectives: Strengths and Weaknesses

Because managing by verifiable objectives and appraisal of managers by results have excited the interest of managers throughout the United States and in many foreign countries, particularly in business enterprises, and because there is far more talk than effective action, it might be helpful to emphasize the major strengths and weaknesses of the system. One cannot overlook the fact, too, that many have tried managing and appraising by objectives, many have failed, some have had only partial success, and only a few companies have really succeeded. The potential of managing and appraising managers by objectives is very great but it is, at best, not a system that can do everything to assure effective management. There is even the danger that the system might degenerate into a management fad or an unsuccessful managerial gimmick.

Strengths of Appraising against Verifiable Objectives

To a very great extent, advantages of appraising against objectives cannot be separated from the benefits of managing by objectives. Clearly, to appraise performance against objectives is to assume that objectives have been established and the person being appraised has been working toward their attainment.

Better Managing The most important advantage of the system is that it can result in much improved managing. Actionable objectives cannot be established without planning and results-oriented planning is the only kind that makes sense. It forces managers to think of planning for *results,* rather than merely planning *activities* or *work.* To assure that objectives are realistic, it also requires the manager to think of the way he will accomplish given results, the organization and personnel he will need to do it, and the resources and interorganizational assistance he will require. Also, there is no better incentive for control and no better way to know what the standards of control are than for a manager to have a clear goal before him.

It is, then, an approach to managing, and not another personnel program added to the burdens of the manager. At the same time, it should not be forgotten that there are other things in managing, and a necessarily limited number of important objectives should not camouflage the other work that must be done.

Seeing management and appraisal by objectives in the total framework of the managerial job shows how it is central to managing and why, if well done, it must help improve the overall performance of a manager. Although all of the interactions and tasks of managing are not directly dealt with, the system does place a heavy emphasis on planning and control, requires support from organization structure and human and material resources, and implies effective leading and directing.

Clarifying Organization   A major strength of a system of managing by objectives is the clarification of organization roles and structure which is almost sure to occur. Objectives must fit key result areas and both, to the extent possible, should be translated into a position that carries responsibility for specific goal accomplishment.

Companies that have seriously embarked on a program of managing by objectives have often discovered organizational deficiencies. The most common is lack of clear delegation of authority which brings the firm face to face with the basic principle of delegation—to delegate by results expected. The resultant decentralization, without loss of control, has changed the organizational system in a number of companies. As an executive of Honeywell is reported to have said: "There are two things that might also be considered fundamental creed at Honeywell: decentralized management is needed to make Honeywell work and management by objectives is needed to make decentralization work."[1]

In other cases companies have found that some positions were not even necessary when no meaningful set of objectives could be established for them. It has been, then, a means of highlighting poor organization, just as appraisal is a means of uncovering inept manning of organizational roles.

An Effective Way to Improve Planning   Perhaps the most important single benefit of managing by verifiable objectives is the direct and inescapable way it tends to make planning more meaningful. Planning is basic to management and the other functions of the manager have little significance without it. Yet every practicing executive knows that today's crises and "fires" will almost invariably push out planning for tomorrow. It is, therefore, a happy thing when a managing

[1] As reported in W. S. Wikstrom, *Managing by—and with—Objectives* (New York: National Industrial Conference Board, Inc., 1968), p. 21.

technique establishes an environment that forces planning.

Any competent system of managing by objectives will do just that. A manager soon finds that he cannot pull goals out of the air, particularly if attainment of them is to be a major basis for appraising him. If actionable objectives are to be set, they must necessarily reflect the planning environment, or premises, facing the manager; they must take into account the resources and assistance needed and available; and they should reflect the ability of the manager to coordinate group action to attain them. Likewise, since objectives of one manager must support those of his superior, the alert boss is not likely to permit his subordinate to establish goals out of phase with, or not contributing to, his own objectives.

As one company noted, its managers up and down the line soon found out that one manager needed to be aware of the goals of other managers. In addition to an understanding of their superior's objectives, and even those at higher levels, and a natural concern with those of their subordinates, managers often found that they had to know the goals and be aware of the progress toward them of counterparts not in their line of command, because accomplishment of their own objectives might depend on what someone in another department was doing. The production manager, for example, would be foolish not to have his goals coordinated with those of marketing or product research and development.

Planning has a close relationship to budgeting for, after all, budgets must in the first instance be plans. Budgets can only be made after objectives and plans to reach them are made. Thus a management-by-objectives program, to the extent that it improves and gives meaning to plans, does the same for budgeting.

Elicits Commitment   One of the great advantages of a system of managing by objectives is that it elicits commitment for performance. No longer is a man just doing work, following instructions, waiting for guidance or decisions; he is now an individual with clearly defined major purposes. What is more, he has had a part in actually setting his objectives, has had an opportunity to put his ideas into planning, now understands his area of discretion—his authority—and has hopefully been able to get a number of decisions from his superiors to assure that he can accomplish his goals.

These are the elements that make for a feeling of commitment. When all these things are done, a man becomes master of his own fate. Anyone who has worked with this system, as the author has, is surprised and pleased to find the seriousness and completeness of this sense of commitment. Top executives ordinarily have it without a system of management by objectives, largely because of their position of influence and their closeness to the end results of a firm. But managers on down the line have not usually had this feeling, and it is they in whom the spark of drive under a well-operated program is so noteworthy, and whose desire to accomplish, or to experience a sense of self-actualization, is so prominent.

Gives the Best Guides and Reasons for Control   One of the frustrating problems in effective control is to know what things to watch and how to select those critical factors in any situation that the manager must watch if he is to be assured that his actions are conforming to plans. The author has been highly critical of typical statistical and other control reports that grind out of modern electronic processing systems miles of paper and yet do not inform managers of what *they* need to know in order to control *their* operations. He has made pleas for years for tailored controls—tailored to the job, to the plan, to the man, and to the needs for effective and efficient controls. In many instances, the very manager who grouses about the poor information he gets is at a loss when the harried information specialists ask him what he needs to know.

In cases of effective management by objectives, this

problem is often solved. Now, the manager knows what he should watch. Now, he has a standard against which to measure his progress. Indeed, there has probably been no development in management that has contributed so much to improving the quality of control.

Appraisal Is Operational   Appraising managers on the basis of their performance against verifiable objectives has the great advantage of being operational. As pointed out in the previous chapter, these appraisals are not something apart from the job a manager does. It is his job. Admittedly, there are difficulties, as outlined earlier. There are always the questions of how well a man did, there are always queries as to whether the goals were missed through no fault of his own, whether the goals were originally set too high or too low, and how many goal attainments are necessary for average or outstanding performance.

But information on what a man has done against what he agreed was a reasonable target is available. Moreover, it is available in an atmosphere of the superior working with and helping his subordinate—not sitting in remote judgment of him.

Weaknesses in the System

With all its advantages, a system of operating and appraising by verifiable objectives has a number of weaknesses which a company or other enterprise should be aware of if it is operating under it or is contemplating doing so. To be aware is to guard against these weaknesses, to supplement the system and its operation with other measures, or to take steps to avoid such deficiencies. A clear distinction should be made between those weaknesses that are found in the system itself and those found so often in practice which alert management could avoid. The following are those that are believed to exist in the system.

Goals Are Difficult to Set   Even with considerable analysis and study, goals with the right degree of "stretch" or "pull" are difficult to set quarter in and quarter out, year in and year out. Dealing with the future and with the inevitable uncertainties involved, it is not easy to set actionable, meaningful goals. This is not really more difficult than any kind of planning, although it takes people more study and work to establish verifiable objectives than to develop most plans, many of which tend only to lay out work.

One of the major problems is getting objectives that are attainable and yet not easily so. However, as mentioned earlier, most people have to be watched by their superior, in the earlier days of the program at least, so that they do not set goals too high. Then, after experience, and where goal achievement becomes the major standard of appraisal and sometimes a determinant of compensation or promotion, there is a natural tendency for subordinates to build padding into goals to assure that they will exceed them.

Tendency of Goals to Be Short Term   In almost all systems of operating under management by objectives, goals are set for the short term, seldom more than a year and often quarterly, or less. There is clearly a danger of emphasizing the short term at the expense of the longer range.

This weakness can be avoided in at least two ways. One is for the superior managers who approve goals to make sure that their subordinates' objectives do not rob the future and that they are consistent with longer-range goals. Another approach, often used in the best systems of managing by objectives, is to have managers, particularly at the middle and upper levels, set longer-term goals. One company, for example, insists on the establishment of five-year objectives in the same verifiable terms that the annual and quarterly objectives are set. Short-term goals are then always, in any goal-setting review, subject to justification as being consistent with five-year goals.

Overemphasis on Objectives Critics of many programs of management by objectives feel that managers get too concerned with the setting and attaining of a few objectives. It is possible that an individual may overlook the other aspects of his job or may push his own objectives at the expense of the company. A production manager, for example, may be so zealous in accomplishing cost reduction goals through making long runs of a product as to defeat inventory goal limitations or the sales manager's desire to have products available at all times. Or the sales manager may be so driven to increase sales that he will concentrate on the easier-to-sell low-profit items.

This is a weakness in the system and it is also a weakness due to poor practice. In the first place, no workable system of objectives can cover every detail of a man's job. Second, it should never be assumed that objectives are independent of each other, within or between departments. They must ever represent a network of interrelated objectives. In the third place, management by objectives is not all there is to managing. It is a tool of managing, not a substitute. In setting goals in particular and in following their progress, every manager is expected to make sure that goals are coordinated, that no phase of the manager's job is neglected, and that constraints, such as inventory limits, are fully recognized.

May Not Really Show Performance One of the great weaknesses in appraising performance against verifiable objectives is that it is entirely possible for an individual to meet or miss goals through no fault of his own. Luck does play a part in performance. It is possible that a new product will take off in the market far beyond expectations and make the sales effort look exceptional, when the quality of the sales program and its implementation were really poor. Or it is possible that unforeseen bad luck will make a manager miss certain of his goals by a considerable margin.

This happens in every company. In one company with a European subsidiary, a drab market performance for several years was suddenly replaced with a brilliant sales record, not because the sales program was any better, but rather because the consumers suddenly "found" the product and it became stylish to have it. In another company, the financial vice-president missed his cash procurement goals considerably because of the generally unforeseen tightening of money supply in 1969.

Most evaluators faced with this problem will say that they take these external and unexpected factors into account in assessing goal performance, and to a very great extent they do. But it is extremely difficult. In an outstanding sales record, for example, how can we be sure how much was due to luck and how much to competence? The outstanding performer is always a "fair-haired boy," at least as long as he performs. The nonperformer likewise cannot escape having a cloud cast over him. The author took pains to watch the future progression of a division manager in one of our largest and best-managed industrial companies who some years ago had a brilliant record of sales growth in his division, largely because of consumer taste changes and style factors over which he had no control. This company had had a long record of thoroughly evaluating managers and taking factors beyond their control into careful consideration in assessing records. While the man was perhaps able, the fact is that, after this period of striking results, his promotion upward to the company presidency was exceptionally rapid.

Appraises Performance Only   Appraisal of performance against objectives obviously only appraises performance. Not only is there the element of luck just mentioned, but there is also the question of other factors to appraise, notably an individual's *managerial* abilities. As has been pointed out earlier, appraisal of performance is not enough, and this is why the author in this book is suggesting a system of supplementing appraisal against objectives by appraising the quality of managing itself. If, as is believed to be the case, the quality of managing makes the difference ultimately in any kind of enterprise, appraisal of performance is just not enough. The star performer tends to rise and then too often to fade.

Danger of Overlooking Individual Development   With its intended emphasis on accomplishing objectives, the system of appraising against objectives may overlook needs for individual development. Objective attainment in practice tends to be short run. Even where longer-range considerations are put into the system, seldom would they be so long range as to contemplate adequate long-term development of managers. The manager concerned with results might really be driven by the system itself to take too little time to plan, implement, and follow through with programs required for the development of his subordinates.

On the other hand, it can be argued that, since performance deficiencies are soon disclosed in an effective system of managing by objectives and that these give a manager better visibility of his subordinates' needs, he can pinpoint development programs better. As possible as this is, if something is to be done, development must be made a part of the system and development goals must be specifically set.

Some people actually do see that performance objectives are supplemented by personal development objectives. The St. Regis Paper Company, for example, requires managers to include among their result areas goals for personnel relationships and for self-development, as well as for development of subordinates. Other, but too few, companies encourage their managers to look for development needs and include programs of this kind in their program goals and appraisals.

Odiorne highlights this deficiency by recommending that

any management-by-objectives program be broadened to include four areas.[2] One is routine duties which he would have measured by merely looking at exceptions. Another area would encompass emergency and problem-solving goals which he would measure by time and the quality of solution. A third kind he refers to as creative goals—those of innovating, creating new methods, and introducing changes for the better—which he would assess by performance against such goals. And the fourth would be personal development goals—such as the development of managerial, behavioral, technical, and professional skills—which can be measured by specific programs of action planned and undertaken.

Weaknesses in Practice

Although no attempt is made here to catalog all the weaknesses that may exist in practice, the author has seen a large number. While the list below may, even so, appear to be forbiddingly long, it is offered as a means of seeing the many practical pitfalls that exist. Basically, as is made abundantly clear in this book, managing and appraising against objectives are a magnificent and productive management technique. It is, nevertheless, like all good approaches to managing, fraught with difficulties. It is a system not easy to install or maintain. But it is one very worthwhile doing well.

Learning the System Is Difficult Despite the unassailable logic of a system of management by objectives, experience has shown that it is not self-teachable and people have some difficulty in learning it. For one thing, those who have been accustomed to planning (if at all) and doing work find

[2] G. S. Odiorne, *Management by Objectives* (New York: Pitman Publishing Corporation, 1965).

it difficult to shift to developing actionable objectives. For another thing, the meaning and practice of verifiability are not easy. Also, it is difficult to set up an entire company or department environment to make the system work. Any enterprise or department starting a program should be happy if it operates reasonably well in three years, and really intelligent results might take longer.

Failure to Teach Its Nature and Philosophy   Because of difficulty in learning the system and the fact that it is usually different from previous practice, many failures result because people who are expected to operate under it do not understand the nature and philosophy of the system. This requires patient explanation of the entire program, what it is, how it works, why it is being done, how appraisal will work, and above all how everyone can benefit from the program.

Many programs have failed for this reason. One of the maladies of managers, particularly those at the top, is the search for the ready and easy solution and then taking a program, such as managing by objectives, getting all the forms and instructions in writing and "installing" it. This will not work. People are accustomed to so-called personnel gimmicks, will give lip service to any program the top boss wants, and will fill out the necessary paper work. Unless there is a complete understanding of what the system is and what the philosophy is underlying it, the paper may flow but the results are not likely to be impressive.

Failure to Give Goal Setters Guidelines   One of the major reasons why management by objectives does not work is, as with other kinds of planning and budgeting, the failure to give goal setters adequate guidelines. These, referred to earlier as planning premises, are essential if an individual is to develop a program and a goal which has any consistency with other programs and goals in an enterprise. People must have some assumptions as to the future, some understanding of company policies and the directions of other plans and objectives in order to do their planning effectively. No one can plan in a vacuum. The question will always be, What does the goal setter fill this vacuum with?

Failure to Tune In on Corporate Objectives   One of the most important of all guidelines for a manager is knowledge of corporate goals and how his activity fits in with their accomplishment. If corporate objectives are fuzzy, unreal, or inconsistent, it is virtually impossible for a manager to tune in with them.

The setting and publication of verifiable corporate goals, even on a preliminary basis and even if they must be modified as changes and possible attainment are recycled in the system, will at least furnish a helpful guide. Identification of key result areas reflecting them will also help. It is obviously wise to have goals throughout the structure that are in tune with corporate goals. Yet this does not just happen. Work, teaching, and open lines of information are necessary.

Failure to Assure a Network of Goals   An important weakness in practice is the failure to assure that goals represent a coordinated, interconnected network. A company is a system. If goals are not interconnected and mutually supportive, people can very often pursue paths that may seem good for their own function but may be detrimental to the company as a whole.

It is sometimes overlooked that planning programs and the goals toward which each is aimed are seldom linear, that is, where something is accomplished, followed by something else, and so on. It is almost universal that programs are interlocking in a network fashion. Chart VI depicts the interlocking network of contributory programs which constitute a typical new product program. Moreover, as can be readily appreciated, each of the interconnected programs shown

Chart VI
NETWORK OF PROGRAMS COMPRISING A TYPICAL
NEW PRODUCT PROGRAM

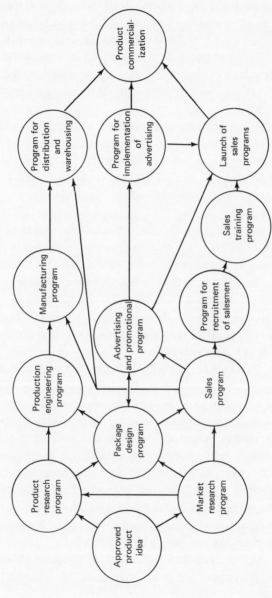

could itself be broken down into an interlocking network. Thus the product research program shown in Chart VI as a single event might involve within it a network of such subsidiary programs as development of a preliminary schematic design, development of a bread-board model, simplifying electronic and mechanical elements, packaging, and other events.

As can be seen, the network of programs and goals places a heavy burden on those making sure that they fit each other. And fitting is not only a matter of having the various programs done, but of timing their completion, since undertaking one program often depends upon completion of another.

It is easy, especially in the earlier stages of management by objectives, for one department to set goals that will seem entirely appropriate for it and will make it look good, only to be operating at cross-purposes with another department. This is partly a weakness in the system with its emphasis on objectives, but it is mostly a weakness in practice since no perceptive manager could overlook the importance of networks in planning.

This failure is closely tied in with lack of understanding and appreciating corporate objectives and other guidelines. It may also be due to poor organization or simply the necessities of complex organization, such as in the development of new products, where many organizational units are usually involved. While we can try to organize along key result areas, this may not be possible. Other factors may be controlling, such as technology—an oil company simply cannot have an integrated gasoline division—or personality considerations— a research engineer seldom likes to see himself as actually a part of the marketing organization.

Many companies only become aware of this problem after some experience with managing by objectives. It is bad enough when goals do not support each other, but it is tragic when they interfere with each other. What is needed, as one company has described it, is a "matrix of mutually supportive goals."

Setting Arbitrary Goals   One of the sure causes of failure is for the principal to set arbitrary goals for his subordinates. His anxiety to turn in a good performance, the authoritative attitude that he knows best, and his wish to avoid the time-consuming process of holding goal-setting sessions might lead a manager to think he is resolving the whole problem by setting the goals himself. But he certainly is not. As a matter of fact, these arbitrary and pressured goals represent one of the major causes for criticism of management by objectives that has been expressed by managers, particularly at the middle and lower levels.

There can be no question that the superior must approve and have the last say on his subordinate's goals. But there is also no question that completely setting goals for subordinates is self-defeating. No one can feel a sense of commitment to those objectives that are handed down to him. He may even feel a sense of resistance that may not be expressed openly but will take the form of excuses or beating the boss at his own game. Arbitrary goal setting is also foolish in that the superior is deprived of the knowledge and experience that his deputy almost always has. This means the boss loses on all scores—motivation, understanding, opportunity for assistance, and ability to make delegation meaningful.

Failure to Insist on Verifiability   The importance of requiring objectives to be verifiable, whether in a quantitative or a qualitative way, has been repeatedly emphasized in this book. The reasons are clear. As simple as this idea is, examination and experience with a large number of plans show many to be deficient on this score.

To be sure, particularly where objectives are of the qualitative kind, it is difficult or impossible to get complete verifiability. But by setting target dates for completion and outlining purposes and characteristics of qualitative program goals, a workable degree of verifiability can be built into them.

Overinsistence on Numbers   At the other extreme of causes for failure in plans is overinsistence on numbers. In these days when quantification tends to be worshipped, there may be too much of a drive to set things in numbers and to make these exclusive measures of performance. We should not forget, as George C. Homans has said: "Data are not nobler because they are quantitative, nor thinking more logical because mathematical. . . . Let us make the important quantitative and not the quantitative important."[3]

One of the prominent companies in the country has a management-by-objectives program that is simply not working, at least at the middle and lower managerial levels, because there is nothing in the goal structure at those levels which is not expressed in numbers. Knowledge of the system and discussions with managers at these levels disclose what one might expect—an overlooking of many qualitative goal areas of great importance to the success of the company's operations.

Use of Inapplicable Standards   Another danger is that a company, in gauging what is good or average or poor performance of a manager, will weigh his performance against standards that are inapplicable to the job. This has happened in some companies, particularly those that have similar operations that are performed in many geographical locations. In one such company, the headquarters office has set standards of performance applicable to all parts of the company throughout the United States. Thus the manager in Southern California is gauged against the same standard targets as the manager in North Dakota, or the one in Georgia.

---

[3] George C. Homans, *The Human Group* (New York: Harcourt, Brace and World, Inc., 1950), p. 22.

A moment's reflection would indicate that national standards in a far-flung operation, even if the operations are quite similar in product output, would probably not be applicable to managers operating in quite dissimilar markets and environments. In the case mentioned here, they almost certainly are not. What is the result? Frustration, resistance, no real sense of commitment, and playing the numbers game with the bosses and the system. It is probably true here as it is almost universally that, when managing becomes a numbers game, the self-preserving and reasonably intelligent subordinate can almost always beat his boss at that game.

The Dangers of Inflexibility   As often reflected in budgeting, some companies are inflexible in not changing objectives during a period of time, normally a year. For a manager to operate toward an obsolete objective is as foolhardy as to have him work to meet an obsolete plan. Objectives, like plans, must maintain a degree of flexibility and must be related to the realities of a given future.

There are reasons for not wishing to change objectives. If objectives can be changed too easily and too much, they cease to be meaningful goals. Also, where other elements of an enterprise are dependent on a given manager accomplishing his objectives in order to accomplish theirs, changing one goal may force changes—or obsolescence of goals and plans—at various places in the network of goals. If, for example, a new plant cannot be completed on schedule, it may upset production, marketing, and other goals. In an airline, the delay in delivery of a new fleet of airplanes can throw into disarray a host of plans and goals for virtually every part of the company.

At the same time, if goals are materially obsolete, there is no sense in not changing them. In one program, a company held a regional sales manager to his original goals after a material portion of his territory was reorganized into another region. The result was disastrous for the sales manager and also brought to all company managers a feeling of disenchantment for the program.

When changes are made, care should be taken to make sure that the changes are not just due to a manager's failure, although, even in this case, those dependent on his goal accomplishment should be alerted to probable failure. Also, where changes are made, they should be approved at a level in a company, or through appropriate consultations, to assure that those in the network can make suitable provision for the change in their goals and plans.

Failure of Adequate Review, Counseling, and Control   One of the dangers in practice is that progress toward goal accomplishment will not be adequately monitored. Particularly where goals cannot be achieved except in a period of a year or more, or where it is the custom of the company to have goal-setting sessions only once a year, there may be a temptation for the principal, for fear of interfering with his deputy, to sit back and not follow up progress during the period.

This can be dangerous to the superior, as well as the company, who may be relying on adequate performance by a subordinate manager. Goal accomplishment should be regularly reviewed, and it even seems that a fairly formal review should be made at least once each quarter. Just as delegation cannot be abdication of responsibility, so also no principal can assume that all is going well with his subordinates' operations.

The superior, as well as the subordinate, should have regular information available to him as to how well a subordinate's goal performance is progressing. He should regularly review progress by personal consultation, and he should make himself available for counseling to help any of his subordinates meet his goals. This is not, and should not be, taking over the task from his subordinate or relieving him of responsibility. It is merely following through his own job as a manager, and most subordinates will welcome follow-up, counseling, assistance with their problems, and help in removing obstructions to their successful performance.

How to Make Appraisal against Objectives Effective

The analysis above of the strengths and weaknesses of entire systems of management by objectives will naturally give clear clues as to how to make the system effective, and by doing so make appraisal effective. Appraisal itself is fairly simple. At the end of six months or a year, a manager need only appraise the quality of his subordinate's goals and his record of achievement, and assess the reasons for deficiencies in either. It is possible that a poor or inadequate review and appraisal of a manager might be made even with a well-operated system of management by verifiable objectives. The supervising manager may not carefully assess the quality of goals set or thoroughly analyze and review performance. It is impossible, however, to make a meaningful appraisal without a sound system.

Appraisal cannot be separated from the system of managing by objectives. Nor should it be. Appraisal is not a separate program. This, indeed, is its great merit.

To summarize how to make an effective system of appraisal against objectives work, a number of items might be mentioned.

1. *Teach the Nature and Philosophy of the Entire System.* Without doing this as a first step, the result will be a fruitless technique without purpose.

2. *Give Managers Adequate Tools.* These include clear organization and adequate delegation of authority, planning premises and other guidelines, an understanding of company

objectives, and a clear comprehension of the superior's goals and problems.

3. *Recognize the Network Nature and Needs of Goals.* Unless goals are seen as an interlocked system, poor coordination will certainly result. This is an urgent task for every superior up the line.

4. *Insist on Verifiability of Objectives.* As difficult as this may be, there is no such thing as an actionable and meaningful goal without the highest possible degree of verifiability. This is also an indispensable element in achieving objective and sound appraisals.

5. *Make Goals Realistic and Attainable.* Goals too easy neither command respect nor elicit the best possible performance. Goals too difficult or impossible of attainment cause frustration, disrespect for the system, and the slovenly habit of missing targets. Perhaps a useable rule of thumb is that the "right" level of attainability exists when 75 percent of goals are achieved.

6. *Recognize Time Spans in Goals.* Some goals should be achieved in a week, others in a month, some in three months, some in a year, and still others for longer periods. Goal setting and accomplishment should not be forced to coincide with accounting periods, but rather with the time span required for attainment.

7. *Make Goal Setting Joint.* Although the superior must have the final word on his subordinates' goals, the process of setting goals should involve the cooperative working together of both. This is the key to intelligent goals and the indispensable feeling of commitment to them.

8. *Be Willing to Change Goals.* When circumstances occur to make a goal obsolete, it should be changed to one realistic and actionable. Care should be taken not to change so often as to lose the integrity of goals, and changes in interlocking objectives should not be made without due notice, considera-

tion, and action to maintain the accuracy and workability of the entire goal network.

9. *Institute and Maintain at Goal-setting and Appraisal Time a Reasonably Formal and Rigorous Review.* In order to give an aura of importance to the setting of goals and preferably also to review of performance, to create an environment where the subordinate will feel compelled to do his utmost in preparation, to provide a means of having technical assistance available, and to make possible decisions on problem areas, an appropriate small group or committee is recommended, with the immediate superior having the approval role in the group.

10. *See Appraisal as Only One Element of the System of Managing by Objectives.* Management by objectives is a way of managing and appraisal is only a part of it. Appraisal in this area of performance, at least, should never be allowed to be regarded as a separate "program."

chapter five

Appraisal of Managers as Managers: a Suggested Program

As encouraging as appraisal of managerial performance against verifiable objectives is and as promising as it is as an operational approach to evaluating people for what they actually do, it still leaves much to be desired. As was stated earlier in this book, no one interested in enterprise success over the long term would want managers who could not perform, nor would they want performers for long in a managerial role who could not manage. Therefore, it has long been the author's belief that the ideal system of appraisal would be one that combines evaluation of performance against verifiable objectives *and* evaluation of performance as a manager.

The program presented here is a first and somewhat experimental step toward the second phase of managerial appraisal. However, it has been tested by presentation to a number of executives in both business and government enterprises. And, above all, it has been tested in the demanding crucible of experience. In one company with three domestic divisions and five wholly owned subsidiaries overseas (in Canada, England, Holland, Australia, and New Zealand), it has been used as a method of appraising middle- and top-level managers for five years. Along with a program of appraising managers against verifiable objectives, the system of appraising managers as managers has not only been the means of evaluating managers but also the means of differentiating between bonuses paid to them.

Various Attempts to Appraise Managers as Managers

A number of companies have recognized the quality of managing, along with performance and traits, as a proper subject of evaluation. Typical of these approaches are the programs of the Hughes Aircraft Company, the St. Regis Paper Company, and the Kimberly-Clark Corporation.

Hughes Aircraft Company, 1954 As early as 1954, the Hughes Aircraft Company installed an appraisal system emphasizing management. As can be seen from Table 5, this company used a brief, but perceptive, form that appraised managers in six areas: planning, organizing, directing, coordinating, controlling, and personal, the last being a trait appraisal. It is interesting that in this approach to appraisal, five of the six areas were strictly managerial in nature, and twenty of twenty-seven items on which managers were asked to appraise had to do with the quality of their managing. In this area, the questions did cover fairly well the major aspects of managing. Although representing an interesting and advanced start, there is no evidence that the approach was further developed or widely used by the company.

TABLE 5 Hughes Aircraft Company Management Appraisal Form, 1954

Name of Appraised _____ Position Title _____
   Last   First   Initial

Payroll Number _____ Department _____ Division _____
   In Present Position Since _____

Step 1: Consider the contents of this individual's position and the results expected of him.
Step 2: PERFORMANCE APPRAISAL: Appraise the individual on each factor in relation to his present position for his performance during the period since his last appraisal. Do not permit your appraisal on one factor to influence your rating on another. Do not be unduly influenced by any single, exceptional occurrence or by recent events or incidents. Place a check (✓) in the box which most properly describes his performance for each factor. If a particular factor is not applicable, so indicate.

RATING:

OUTSTANDING	SUPERIOR	SATISFACTORY	FAIR	UNSATISFACTORY
Approaches the best possible for the position	Exceeds normal requirements of assignment	Meets reasonable expectations of position full requirements of position	Below essential requirements of position	Inadequate to fulfill present assignment

Area	FACTOR	DEFINITION	Otsg	Sup	Sat	F	Uns	NA
PLAN	PLANNING	Plans objectives and activities ahead; provides a logical and effective course of action for his group and himself to see that established goals are achieved.						
PLAN	CREATIVENESS	Conceives new creative ideas and techniques; visualizes and anticipates new problems; develops practical solutions.						
PLAN	ADAPTABILITY	Alters his activities to the proper course of action to meet the changing demands of new situations.						
ORGANIZING	ORGANIZATION	Defines and arranges his activity into logical and practical assignments to attain the desired objectives.						
ORGANIZING	DELEGATION	Assigns appropriate responsibilities to subordinates with the authority to develop and execute their designated duties.						
ORGANIZING	TRAINING	Selects good subordinates; arouses their interest and ambitions; appraises their performance and strengthens their weaknesses through counsel and guidance so that they are effective in their present assignments and develop their capabilities for advancement.						
ORGANIZING	LEADERSHIP	Inspires others; stimulates and guides subordinates so that they work together toward common objectives; discovers and utilizes their capabilities; awards recognition for good work.						
DIRECT	JUDGMENT	Develops logical conclusions through sound reasoning of available data; recognizes the significant from the less significant.						
DIRECT	DECISION-MAKING	Makes decisions willingly and promptly; accepts responsibility for his decisions; makes minor decisions well; makes major decisions well.						
DIRECT	ANALYSIS	Studies and examines problems; properly distinguishes their component parts and their separate relationships to the whole.						
DIRECT	APPLICATION	Maintains performance, even in periods of difficult going, in order to accomplish what is undertaken.						
DIRECT	INITIATIVE	Acts independently without specific instructions in an aggressive, self-confident manner.						
DIRECT	EXPRESSION	Organizes and presents his ideas or the results of his activities in a clear and effective oral and written form.						
COORD.	COORDINATION	Blends the efforts of the component functions of his assignment; harmoniously fits his assignment with other components of the organization into an integrated company effort.						
COORD.	LIMITATION	Conducts his function within the scope of his assigned responsibilities and authority.						
COORD.	COOPERATION	Harmoniously works with others, whether subordinates, equals or superiors, in attaining established goals; uses tact and diplomacy in dealing with others.						
CONTROL	CONTROL	Sees that plans are effectively carried out; maintains an awareness of their current status; maintains full mastery of his operations.						
CONTROL	ACCOMPLISHMENT	Achieves assignment with the manpower, materials and facilities allocated and within the goals established; demonstrates an awareness of costs and strives for the most economic utilization of such allocables.						
CONTROL	THOROUGHNESS	Produces work that is comprehensive in scope and complete in detail.						
CONTROL	ACCURACY	Produces work that is free from mistake or error.						
PERSONAL	KNOWLEDGE	Commands those factors or skills essential to his assignment; keeps informed on current developments in his field; maintains familiarity with the company organization, policies and procedures.						
PERSONAL	INTELLIGENCE	Evidences capabilities to think and learn, to grasp ideas, of alertness and resourcefulness.						
PERSONAL	INTEGRITY	Practices honesty, fairness and moral vigor in character and action; is not false to a trust.						
PERSONAL	RELIABILITY	Can be depended upon to fulfill the responsibilities of his position, and in matters of a highly important or confidential nature.						
PERSONAL	STABILITY	Maintains mental and emotional balance under stress due to pressure of work, counter-influence or discouragement.						
PERSONAL	INTEREST	Evidences enthusiasm in his work.						
PERSONAL	HEALTH	Condition of his health, physical endurance and vitality (based on personal observation).						

Step 3: OVER-ALL PERFORMANCE: Appraisal factors vary in importance between different managerial positions. Check (✓) the rating which most nearly describes the individual's over-all performance in his present position during the appraisal period:

- [ ] OUTSTANDING – Consistently approaches the best performance possible.
- [ ] SUPERIOR – Consistently exceeds the reasonable expectations of his position.
- [ ] SATISFACTORY – Consistently meets the requirements of his position; occasionally exceeds or fails to meet these requirements.
- [ ] FAIR – Does not completely meet normal expectations; frequently fails to meet the requirements of his position.
- [ ] UNSATISFACTORY – Inadequate to fulfill present assignment.

Step 4: EVALUATION

1. How could the individual's performance be improved? _____

2. Is the individual well-suited to the type of work in his present assignment? YES [ ] NO [ ] If not, what recommendation do you make? _____

3. Has there been any marked change in the individual's performance since his last appraisal? YES [ ] NO [ ] Explain briefly: _____

4. Is the individual obtaining the breadth of experience necessary for his advancement? YES [ ] NO [ ] If not, what recommendation do you make? _____

5. What course of action do you recommend for the individual during the next year to improve his performance in his present assignment and to prepare him for future advancement?

[ ] Performance in present position	EXPERIENCE		EDUCATION	
	[ ] Technical	[ ] Administrative	[ ] Management Courses	[ ] Coaching
	[ ] Operating	[ ] Special Assignment	[ ] Technical Courses	[ ] On-the-job
		[ ] Other		[ ] Self-Improvement [ ] Other

Explain each item checked: _____

6. Remarks: _____

_____   _____   _____   _____
Appraiser's Signature   Date   Appraiser's Supervisor's Signature   Date

_____   _____
Position Title   Position Title

Step 5: The completed Managerial Appraisal should be reviewed by the appraiser's supervisor.

Step 6: Forward under proper cover the original and the duplicate copy of the completed Managerial Appraisal to the designated Division/Activity office. The duplicate copy will remain on record there and the original transmitted to the Management Development Office.

105

Kimberly-Clark Corporation, 1959   Kimberly-Clark is especially interesting because of its outstanding work toward improving the quality of managing. It is probably the first major company to establish a formal Department of Management Research and Development to undertake special investigation and possible development of management techniques in the same way that the product R&D department does with new products. This move was especially gratifying when one considers how few managerial inventions still exist in the world and how the few techniques that have been invented—such as variable budgeting, the Gantt chart, and network planning (PERT/CPM)—have improved the efficiency of management performance.

This research and development approach led the company into a management-by-objectives program. It also led to an attempt to set up a concept of what managing is by devising "The Management Wheel," reproduced in Chart VII. As can be seen, this wheel groups twenty-four elements of managing under the four areas of planning, organizing, leading, and controlling. It was intended to be used only as a teaching tool, and there is no evidence that it has been used in a formal way for appraisal. However, it was employed as a regular reminder to practicing managers in their daily work, and it has not been unusual for company managers to have it constantly before them.

The company's approach and purpose have much that is commendable. A major purpose was to avoid overemphasis on objectives. While insisting on setting them as a logical first step in managing, the company desired to emphasize the importance of the entire management process. The company refers to this as not managing subordinates but rather "managing their managing." In other words, the superior's task is to make certain that his subordinates have considered not only objectives but also the other "spokes" of the wheel.

Chart VII
THE MANAGEMENT WHEEL

Kimberly-Clark Corporation

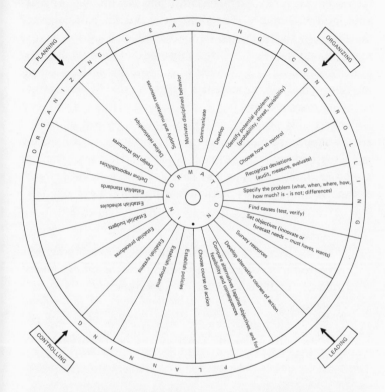

From W. S. Wikstrom, *Managing by—and with—Objectives* (New York: National Industrial Conference Board, Inc., 1968), p. 63.

St. Regis Paper Company, 1967[1]   Another program worthy of note is that developed by the St. Regis Paper Company in 1967. Although the program was primarily based on managing by objectives, a special evaluation was made of man-

[1] As reported in W. S. Wikstrom, *Managing by—and with—Objectives* (New York: National Industrial Conference Board, Inc., 1968), pp. 38–56.

power planning that summarized accomplishments in major result areas, included an "appraisal of methods," brief comments on personal characteristics and health and appearance, and a summary. The summary asked in particular for areas where the manager had accomplished most and the management methods he used most skillfully, as well as the major areas where he planned to concentrate in the succeeding year and the management methods he should concentrate on using more effectively.

Because this program combines both appraisal of performance against verifiable results and an appraisal of management methods, it may be well to summarize the content of the latter. Each manager was asked to comment on his subordinate's management methods in the following areas:

1. *Planning*
   Forecasting; establishing written objectives; programs to accomplish objectives; budgeting; scheduling; allocation of time; involvement of subordinates.

2. *Organizing*
   Staffing; job assignments; clarity of staff's responsibilities and authorities; delegation; and working relationships.

3. *Leading*
   Managing through objectives; initiating action; decision making; communications skill; leadership style; encouragement of expression; resolving conflict situations; gaining cooperation.

4. *Motivating*
   Encouragement of self-development; appraisal and coaching; utilization of skills and abilities of subordinates; attitudes and morale of group; reaction to changes.

5. *Controlling*

Ways used to measure results; scope of measures; use of objectives, targets, budgets, and policies to measure results; corrective action taken.

To aid managers in understanding how to appraise the quality of managing, the company prepared and distributed to key people a booklet, *Guidelines for Managing,* which was really a brief summary of basic principles of management. The company preferred the term "guidelines" to "principles," even though they are really the latter, for fear that the term "principles" would imply rigidity rather than practical application in the light of experience and judgment.

The St. Regis program, based on a company expression of guidelines, a system of managing by objectives of a highly precise nature, and an attempt to force appraisal of "management methods," was certainly on the right track. The major criticism that could be made of this advanced program is that the management appraisal portion of the system was still rather general, calling only for comments in rather broad areas. Such comments might or might not be very perceptive and objective. In fact, they are highly unlikely to be. What the system seemed to need was a larger number of checkpoints for verifiable or at least definite response than were used. This has been done in the objectives section of appraisal, even to the point of structuring them under such specific categories as "quality," "cost," "safety," "sales volume," and "sales expense." It would seem that more specificity might have been helpful in the area of managing.

The Trend toward Emphasizing Managing The few examples quoted above are indicative of what might be expected. As all kinds of enterprises have awakened to the importance of managing and the appropriate use in practice of sound principles and the crude, but helpful and important, science of management, one should expect that the most alert ones would add an appraisal of managers as managers to the already valuable appraisal against verifiable objectives. A number of companies are attempting to do this, at least to some extent, but the standards thus far for appraising managers as managers have seemed to be too broad and too susceptible to general and subjective judgment.

What to Use as Standards for Appraising Managing as Managing

It has been the author's position for many years that the most appropriate standards to be used for appraising managers as managers are the fundamentals of management. It is not enough to appraise a manager on how well he generally undertakes his broad functions of planning, organizing, staffing, directing (or leading and motivating), and controlling. These terms, while important, are too general to be used as standards of appraisal. To do as the St. Regis Paper Company did and give these terms some meaning by specifics is a help. But we should go further.

The best approach the author has found is to utilize the basic principles of management as standards. If they are basic, as it is sincerely believed they are and as they have been found to be in a wide variety of managerial positions, and in a wide variety of cultures, both within the United States and in many foreign countries, they should serve as reasonably good standards. To be sure, their application to situations in practice will vary and results may look different. But this should not bother us. A house built in the Arctic will look quite different from that built in the tropics, but both will utilize the same mechanical and electrical principles.

Also, a manager may design around or disregard principles in order to get a desired result, but the intelligent manager will do so knowing the costs of disregarding them and will make his decision on the grounds that the end results justify any resulting costs. Thus we may readily give the corporation controller specific line-type authority (functional authority or supervision) to direct people not reporting to him to handle accounting and financial matters in a certain way and in accordance with certain policies. This *is* disunity of command. It may cause confusion and diffusion of responsibility, but the end results may justify doing so. This is really no different from what a design engineer does. He may not pick the cheapest, lightest, most ductile, or most conductive of materials, but he will select that combination that gives him the best *total* result desired.

As crude as the basic principles of management may be and as much judgment as may be required for their appropriate use in practice, they do give the evaluator some benchmarks to determine whether his subordinates understand and are following out the functions of managing. Even though application of principles that underly the managerial functions to an individual manager's operations requires a degree of subjective judgment, this is far more meaningful than the more general questions so often used as standards for appraisal. They are definitely more specific than evaluations based on such broad standards as work habits, integrity, cooperation, judgment, intelligence, or loyalty. They at least focus attention on what may be expected of a manager *as a manager*. And, when taken in conjunction with the performance of plans and goals, they can help remove much of the weakness in many present managerial appraisal systems.

An Overall Program of Appraising Managers as Managers

The program for appraising managers as managers suggested here is admittedly tentative and subject to change and improvement. But it has been clinically tested and changes have been made in the light of experience. Moreover, experience with it has shown some of the advantages as well as the disadvantages and pitfalls.

In brief, the program involves breaking down the functions of the manager into planning, organizing, staffing, directing, and controlling, in accordance with the book of which the writer is co-author.[2] Then each function is dealt with in a series of questions designed to reflect the most important fundamentals of managing in each area. The total list of key questions, the form used, the system of ratings, and the instructions that have been given with the form may be found in Appendix 2. In the following sections of this chapter, each managerial function and the checkpoints applicable to each will be dealt with in detail. Later, the means of rating will be discussed.

It was first hoped to make the rating completely objective by designing the checkpoints and the questions to be "go-no-go," that is, the manager being rated either did it or did not. Regretfully, this was not found to be possible. Degrees of "how well" had to be inserted. To make these degrees as explicit as possible and to avoid the natural tendency of managers not to discriminate in their item-by-item appraisal, several things were done. In the first place, the concept of degree was sharply defined. Second, in the final appraisal summary rating, managers were asked to give examples of very high or very low ratings. In the third place, managers were informed that a portion of their rating by their superior would assess the intelligence and discrimination they showed in evaluating their subordinates. And finally, the superior's superior was required to review ratings and make his appraisal of the quality of ratings.

In the major clinical test, appraisal of managers as mana-

[2] H. Koontz and C. O'Donnell, *Principles of Management*, 4th ed. (New York: McGraw-Hill Book Company, 1968).

gers was tied to a program of accomplishing verifiable objectives. These two appraisals were then the major determinants (along with position and salary level) of annual bonus award variations between managers in the top and middle levels of the company. The reader may be assured that in bonus recommendations and in the final allocation of bonuses by the bonus committee of the board of directors, these appraisals were given careful consideration and definitely affected bonus award variances.

Because of the problem of semantics and the varying degrees of understanding in management concepts, the author's jointly written book *Principles of Management* was used as the authoritative reference. Naturally other companies might want to use another book. Some may wish, as the St. Regis Paper Company did in their system, to write their own manual on the concepts and principles of management. Whatever is done, some source of authoritative definition is necessary. Even in a small, closely knit company, managers will ordinarily vary considerably in their understanding of concepts and principles. In a far-flung company and especially one operating both in the United States and overseas, the differences can be considerable.

In the following analysis of these checkpoints, the Koontz and O'Donnell book is used as a reference. For those who may wish to check this out in greater detail, applicable pages from *Principles of Management* (4th ed.) are cited after most of the checkpoints. As a matter of fact, for easy reference of the managers operating under this plan, this was done in practice.

Appraising Managers as Managers: Planning

The following checkpoints have been selected to indicate managerial competence in planning. They are not meant to be exhaustive but to represent critical points that indicate the manager's understanding and competence in applying the basics of managerial planning.

1. *Does he set for his departmental unit both short-term and long-term goals in verifiable terms (either quantitative or qualitative) that are related in a positive way to those of his superior and his company?*[3] (Pp. 84–85, 94, 111–121, 484–501.)

This question is fairly self-explanatory. The emphasis is on the setting of verifiable goals or objectives and in making sure that they are related to those of his principal and his company and that the maker considers long-run implications as well as short-run influences.

2. *To what extent does he make sure that the goals of his department are understood by those who report to him?* (Pp. 120–121.)

Adequate understanding of a superior's goals requires not only a clear statement of them and discussion with subordinates, but a clear understanding of the premises that underlie such objectives and an explanation of the reasoning that led to them. Understanding of objectives and their environment, plus participation of the subordinate in setting his own and relating these to his superior's objectives, are the best assurance of understanding and loyalty to goals. Everyone likes to understand what part he is playing in a game. This is nowhere more important than in setting objectives.

3. *How well does he assist those who report to him in establishing verifiable and consistent goals for their operations?* (Pp. 120–121.)

Participation in setting goals is one of the best assurances that a subordinate will develop meaningful goals and a sense of commitment to their attainment. He also needs the assis-

[3] While "company" is used, the reader should understand that the questions apply equally to nonbusiness operations.

tance of his superior beyond advice and help in understanding the environment of plans. Aid should be expanded to making sure that human and material resources will be available, that obstructions to performance are removed to the extent possible, and that supporting decisions are in fact made. What most people want is an opportunity to perform, to accomplish. But this cannot exist if there is lack of understanding, obstructions, inadequate tools and resources, and key decisions hanging fire.

4. *To what extent does he utilize consistent and approved planning premises in his planning and see that his subordinates do likewise?* (Pp. 94–96, 123–151.)

The importance of planning premises has been emphasized in earlier pages of this book. But acceptable assumptions for the future are seldom made clear to those, particularly below the top levels, who must do so much of the action planning in an enterprise. Moreover, if planning is to be sound and fit in with the total network of plans, these premises must be consistent and should represent those approved by the company. The importance of consistency is fairly obvious; it does not make sense for one segment of plans to proceed on one set of assumptions and another on a different set. Also, because so many planning premises involve forecasts of the future and these are subject to error, the critical premises should be approved at or near the top of the company as representing the set of future expectations the company is willing to stand by.

5. *Does he understand the role of company policies in his decision making and assure that his subordinates do likewise?* (Pp. 85–89, 177–197.)

Policies are designed to give structure to plans, to permit delegation of authority but set reasonable bounds to its exercise. The essence of policy is discretion. The function of policies is to mark out an area of discretion where decisions can be made, where actions can be taken. They cover virtually every sphere of a company's operation. They may permit a broad range of discretion or a narrow one, but when the area of discretion allowed disappears, that which is often called policy becomes, in fact, a rule.

Written or unwritten, understood or not understood, all enterprises have policies. If planning at various points in an enterprise is to be done with any degree of consistency and integrity, policies must be understood. Moreover, experience in many companies has shown that when people understand the content and meaning of policies, they can and will be encouraged not only to make decisions but to make them within desired bounds and in accordance with desired directions. It is, consequently, of the utmost importance that superiors understand policies and that they make sure their subordinates do likewise.

6. *Does he attempt to solve problems of subordinates by policy guidance, coaching, and encouragement of innovation, rather than by rules and procedures?* (Pp. 85–89, 215.)

One of the surest signs of a poor manager is his attempt to solve too many problems by establishing procedures or rules. Both of these spell out courses of specific action or nonaction. Neither, in essence, allows the exercise of discretion. For those who want to make sure that their deputies make no mistakes, the most certain way is to promulgate a rule or establish a procedure. But when this is done, there can be no room for significant planning.

This is not to say that rules and procedures should never be established and are always unwise. There are many instances where we want things done in a certain way either to control action or because we have found the most efficient way of doing something and there would be waste in allowing everyone to find out for himself how to do it. This is the case with many accounting system requirements or factory assembly techniques. However, what managers do at times is to set up a bureaucratic system for assuring that things will be done in a certain way, when actually the problem would better be solved by allowing people discretion, within established policy, and opportunities for innovative approaches through working out the best course of action themselves.

7. *Does he help his subordinates get the information they need to assist them in their planning?* (Pp. 200–201.)

The best planning occurs when everyone has access to complete information affecting the area of planning for which he is responsible. It is the job of the superior to help his subordinates get this information if they cannot otherwise obtain it. This may mean opening doors, making reports available, or actually getting it for subordinates. There are, of course, limits to the amount of information any manager can get concerning a specific program. There are limits of time, ability to absorb, availability, and requirements imposed by business secrecy, although the last is often exaggerated. Competitors sometimes have information on a "confidential" business matter when people in an enterprise who need it do not.

Nevertheless, inadequacy of information—to be distinguished from the sheets of data that do not inform—is perhaps one of the major deterrents to effective planning. Not only does information help those who must plan to come up with a more intelligent and meaningful course of action, but by leading to understanding it can go far in eliciting trust and enthusiasm.

8. *To what extent does he seek out applicable alternatives before making a decision?* (Pp. 152–153.)

It is easy for anyone to fall into the trap of jumping to conclusions, of assuming that there is only one way to do something. It is a pretty safe rule of life that, when there seems only one way to do something, that way is wrong. The intelligent decision maker will always look for applicable alternatives.

In the dynamic operations of today, however, the problem is likely to be that there are so many ways a thing could be done that we wish some would go away. Even with operations research techniques and the computer allowing us to analyze a large number of alternatives in many areas, we seldom can look at every possible one. Where it is not practicable to utilize these techniques, the decision maker has an even more difficult task: that of picking out the relatively few most applicable approaches to solving a problem and solving by analyzing these in terms of the goal sought. This is a virtually indispensable managerial skill.

9. *In choosing from among alternatives, does he recognize and give primary attention to those factors which are limiting or critical to the solution of a problem?* (Pp. 153–155.)

There is probably no greater skill in decision making than the ability to utilize what is called the principle of the limiting, or critical, factor. In every problem situation there are a few variables that make the most difference in the solution. Thus, in an advertising program, the critical factor might be limitation of funds available; or in developing a new product, it might be the availability of a low-cost reliable component. If we cannot recognize and solve the limiting or critical factor, we cannot solve the problem.

In practical problem solving, it is often difficult to distinguish the critical factor from other variables since there are other variables that may have an effect on an answer. Normally, we cannot study every variable with an influence on an answer. We may not have the time or the resources to do so.

This skill of the effective decision maker does not necessarily bear any relationship to high intelligence. Some of the most intelligent and highly trained scientists may not possess it. In fact, as every manager knows who has dealt with them, many of these highly intelligent individuals can spend an almost infinite amount of time and resources studying every variable, its nature, and its impact on an answer. Searching for the limiting factor or factors and solving for it may not give the perfect answer, but the decision maker who does so will not suffer from what has been called "paralysis from analysis."

10. *In making decisions, how well does he bear in mind the size and length of commitment involved in each decision?* (Pp. 99–104.)

Every decision involves some commitment of resources, direction, or reputation for some period of time in the future. In some, the commitment can be fulfilled, or missed, in a matter of minutes or days. In others, for example, in building a special-purpose facility such as an oil refinery, we may not get our dollar bills back for many years. On the other hand, some commitments may be for small expenditures or for relatively unimportant matters.

While a manager's area of discretion, embodied in his authority to commit, should be suitable to his level of responsibility in an organization, this is not always the case. Whatever the limits of authority, or discretion, are, the effective manager should be assessed on the basis of whether he realizes and appropriately bears in mind the size and length of commitment involved in every decision he makes. That this may be difficult is indicated by the example where a first-line supervisor thoughtlessly made certain personnel decisions that led to bringing into a once friendly and family-type company a vigorous and difficult labor union.

11. *Does he check his plans periodically to see if they are consistent with current expectations?* (Pp. 105–106.)

Plans are always made on the basis of some set of expectations of the future. If these change materially, it may well be that the plans will become obsolete. The effective manager is like a navigator. He lays out plans as to how the ship or airplane is to travel between two points, but he takes readings from time to time to see if it is off course and makes changes in his plans so that the objective may be reached, or in certain circumstances, he is forced to change the objective.

12. *To what extent does he consider the need for, as well as the cost of, flexibility in arriving at a planning decision?* (Pp. 104–106, 224.)

Because of unavoidable uncertainties in the future, the effective manager will always wish to consider the possibilities of building elements of flexibility—a means of changing direction without undue cost or difficulty—into a program of any consequence. It is true that the most inflexible plan is almost certainly the least costly. A special-purpose machine or building will be more efficient than one designed for general purposes. A specific program of action with no hedges will be the least expensive. But they are only so if the purpose for which they are designed or the environment on which they are premised does not change.

Therefore, except for unimportant decisions, the astute manager will wish to consider building flexibility into his program. But he must consider the cost. Is it worth it? Moreover, there are some decision areas where it may be virtually impossible to provide for flexibility. An oil-gathering pipeline system in an oil field or a refinery in a given area is only useful for handling petroleum. Clearly, where a program is by its very nature highly inflexible, the size and length of a commitment deserve special attention.

13. *In developing and implementing his plans, does he regularly consider longer-range implications of his decisions*

along with the shorter-range results expected? (Pp. 99–104, 221.)

To some extent, this checkpoint is similar to item 10 above. But it is more specific and deals with habits that become so easily ingrained in practicing managers. Partly because of our being wedded to accounting and budgetary periods of time and partly because people are likely to be far more concerned with today's problems, it is important to emphasize the necessity of seeing, and planning for, the longer-range implications of shorter-range plans.

Too often, short-range plans are made without reference to long-range programs. Many short-range programs are really meant to contribute to the achievement of some long-range plan. Many of the errors and wastes of planning arise because decisions are taken on current problems without considering the effect on longer-range objectives.

14. *When he submits problems to his superior, or when a superior seeks help from him in solving problems, does he submit considered analyses of alternatives (with advantages and disadvantages) and recommend definite suggestions for solution?* (Pp. 293–294, 324.)

As every manager knows, there are problem finders (or, sometimes, creators) and problem solvers. The higher one goes up the structure of organization, the more problems lie on executives' desks and the fewer answers. Recently, in a period of six months, the chief executives of four different companies asked the author how they could stop "delegation upward"—the resubmission to them of problems that they had thought they had delegated downward. The soundest approach is not to let problems come back up, refuse to entertain them, or at least insist that the problem submitters accompany problems with an analysis of alternatives and a thoroughly thought out recommendation for action.

It is this quality in a subordinate that endears him to his boss, with the possible exception of the autocrat who wants to make all the decisions himself without help. If this "upward push" for problem solutions is an important attribute of a subordinate, then it should certainly be one of the things on which he should be evaluated. Moreover, the deputy who does this for his principal is likely to encourage such action from his subordinates.

Appraising Managers as Managers: Organizing

Organizing is regarded as the function of a manager that has to do with establishing an intentional structure of roles. As will be recalled from the first chapter, a role must include verifiable goals, as well as a defined area of discretion, a knowledge of principal duties (result areas), and an understanding of informational relationships. But organization is structure, a network of roles which can most effectively and efficiently contribute to the attainment of enterprise objectives. It is, of course, affected by the company's environment —economic, technical, social-cultural, political, and ethical. No one with an ounce of sense would think of designing an organization structure without considering such influences. It must come as a great surprise to practicing managers and management consultants that in recent years certain researchers have "discovered" that technology affects organization.

In defining the functions of the manager, the task of staffing—the manning of the structure through selection, training, appraisal, and compensating its incumbents—is separated from that of organizing. This is not meant to imply that organizing can be done without reference to the people available to fill roles, although it is well recognized that the good organizer starts with the ideal structure and *then* modifies it for people. The principal reason for separating staffing is to emphasize the importance of this function and its peculiarities, an emphasis of real importance when so many managers have tended to relegate this task wholly to personnel departments.

To appraise this area of managing, the author has found that nineteen checkpoints or key questions can cover the essentials.

1. *Does the organization structure under his control reflect major result areas?* (Pp. 232–239.)

This question hardly needs elaboration. As pointed out earlier in the book, a company or any of its departments exists to accomplish certain important results. It may not be possible in every case to organize a single department or section around a key result area. Also, as one goes down the line, an individual manager's power to control structure may be limited. However, to the extent that a manager can organize so that a unit takes charge of given key results, he should be appraised on his ability and willingness to do so effectively.

2. *Does he delegate authority to his subordinates on the basis of results expected of them?* (P. 75.)

This is the first principle of delegation. It is simple, but it is important. Too often delegation is looked upon as parcelling out authority, instead of what it really is—the allocation of an area of discretion necessary for a person to accomplish his goals.

3. *Does he make his delegations clear (rather than detailed)?* (Pp. 68–69, 407–408, 417–421.)

One of the major faults of managing in practice is that delegations are not clear, are not understood by the recipient or by others with whom he must work. This error, probably more than most others, accounts for organizational frictions, jealousies, and inefficiencies. Lack of clarity causes lack of knowledge of an individual's role in an organization. Yet clarity of delegation or assignment should not be confused with the tendency to spell a job out in too much detail, to build into it a web of specifics and restrictions. It does not mean restriction of role where restriction is not desired or necessary. Detailed delegations or assignments may result unwittingly in building an unintended straitjacket around a job. It is far more difficult to be clear without being detailed, but it is the hallmark of good delegation.

4. *Does he formalize in writing his subordinates' position guides, authority delegations, and goals?*

Putting position guides, authority delegations, or goals in writing will not assure that they will be thought out or clear. But if they are not in writing, one can almost be sure that they will be unclear, will be misunderstood by others, and may be forgotten at the time of performance appraisal.

5. *Does he clarify responsibilities for contributions to his programs?*

Because organization in accordance with result areas and authority delegations can seldom reflect the dynamic characteristics of ongoing programs, a manager must take special care to make sure that, for each program for which he needs his subordinates' contributions and coordinated actions, program responsibilities are clarified.

6. *Does he maintain adequate control when delegating authority?* (Pp. 66, 374–375.)

This checkpoint might equally well be included under the function of control. It is listed here in order to emphasize the fact that a principal may assign duties and delegate some of his authority, but he cannot delegate his responsibility to his superior. Delegation is not abdication of responsibility. The only answer to assure discharge of his responsibility without interfering with a delegation is for the principal to devise and utilize methods of control that will tell him how well the deputy is doing in exercising his delegated authority.

7. *Does he exact commensurate responsibility when he delegates authority?* (P. 409.)

A corollary to delegation of authority is the exaction of responsibility, the obligation to perform properly in accordance with a delegation. This is an aspect of the maintenance of control involved in the previous point. But it is more. It anticipates that the superior will undertake such means and establish such a climate that the subordinate will be required to feel and discharge his obligation to perform in accordance with a delegation.

8. *When he has delegated authority to his subordinate, does he refrain from making decisions in that area?* (Pp. 71, 74.)

One of the major causes of failure on the part of a manager, especially in a growing enterprise or when he is promoted to a higher position, is for him to delegate in name only and continue to make decisions in the area delegated to his subordinate. To do so is obviously to negate the delegation. It should, therefore, be a key area to be watched and appraised.

9. *Does he take steps to make sure that his subordinates are properly delegating their authority where necessary?* (Pp. 368–375.)

Just as it is important that a superior delegate appropriate authority to his subordinates, it is likewise important that they, in turn, delegate necessary authority to their deputies. Many a program of effective delegation has been rendered worthless by having the organizational authority lead to a dead end — a manager who refuses to delegate to those reporting to him. This requires careful and perceptive surveillance by every manager.

10. *Does he maintain unity of command or disregard it only when the advantages of doing so clearly offset the disadvantages?* (Pp. 74–75.)

It is sometimes argued that the principle of unity of command is not true because it is so often disregarded in practice. This is not so and derives from a misunderstanding of what the principle really is. The principle is that the more an individual reports to a single superior, the less likely that there will be confusion in instructions, guidance, and expectations, and the more an individual will feel a sense of loyalty and responsibility to his superior.

In other words, the principle of unity of command, like other principles, does not imply that an action should never be taken. Rather, it says that if disunity is built into an organization, one can expect certain costs. There are many cases where disunity may be unavoidable or where the total end result justifies it. As mentioned before, this is certainly the case where the corporate controller is given a special kind of authority in accounting matters over people who do not report to him. What is a desirable standard of managing is not that multiple command should never occur, but that a manager should be aware of the costs and resort to it only where the benefits outweigh them.

11. *Does he utilize staff advice when necessary, and then only as advice?* (Pp. 296–297.)

Staff is one of those long-confused areas of management. It is sometimes forgotten that staff is nothing more than an advisory relationship built into an organizational role. Where wisely provided, it is there to help the manager in a line role do a better and more informed job. It is there to assist and not to dictate, and it must be the responsible manager's responsibility, and his only, to decide whether staff advice is accepted.

12. *Does he regularly teach to his subordinates, or otherwise make sure that his subordinates understand, the nature of line and staff relationships?* (Pp. 291–301, 321–325.)

Because of misunderstanding of these concepts and the problems that arise in practice, one of the important contributions to effectiveness a manager can make is to be sure his subordinates understand and apply in practice basic line and staff relationships. As indicated above, staff is that element in an organizational role that is advisory, while line is that element that is supervisory.

13. *Does he limit and make crystal clear to his departments the functional authority delegations in writing?* (Pp. 301–309, 317, 409–410.)

One of the hybrid arrangements found so often in organization that causes confusion and difficulties is the existence of functional authority or functional supervision. This is the authority an individual may have delegated to him over specified processes, practices, policies, or other matters relating to activities undertaken by personnel in departments other than his own. The previously noted case of the controller's authority in accounting matters is a case in point.

Seldom are these functional authorities spelled out and made clear, although the demands of modern organization make them unavoidable in many instances. There is ample evidence that the lack of understanding of functional authority leads to much confusion and undesirable frictions and wastes. To avoid these problems, at least in large part, clarification of functional authority is an essential step.

14. *Does he use service departments only when it is clear that control is required or efficiency will be enhanced beyond the costs and dangers of inadequate service?* (Pp. 343–345.)

Service departments are groupings of activities, that might logically be carried on in the departments these activities serve, into a special department for purposes either of control or efficiency, or both. Accounting is an activity that *could* be carried on in every department, but is usually concentrated both for control and efficiency. Plant maintenance may be placed in a special department primarily for efficiency.

Electronic data-processing activities, stenographic services, and personnel recruitment are often similarly grouped in a single department for purposes of efficiency.

Sometimes, however, this efficiency is illusory. The service itself may be performed at a low cost but often other operations suffer from inadequate, slow, or incompetent aid. The trouble is that savings of costs in concentrating activities can almost always be proved, but the costs and problems for those being served are extremely difficult to calculate. Proper use of this device of organization is, therefore, worth appraising.

15. *Does he take care not to create excessive levels of organization?* (Pp. 243–245, 252–254.)

The more levels of organization created, the greater the expense and the more filtering of communications, either up or down, that results. Yet levels are necessary to avoid the costs of excessive spans of management. While the proper span cannot be precisely stated numerically, but depends on managers and many underlying variables, too narrow spans are certainly to be avoided. The ultimate of the narrow span is the utilization of a line assistant where the manager has only one person reporting directly to him. While this may sometimes be justified, these cases are likely to be rare.

16. *Does he exercise care not to use committees or group meetings to make decisions that could better be made by individuals?* (Pp. 389–391, 397–399.)

While there are some decisions that should be made by committees or groups, primarily those matters of great importance, required by law, or of great sensitivity, there can be no doubt that modern organized enterprise uses them far too much. Unfortunately, too, committees properly set up as advisory and deliberative bodies of great value to the practicing executive may slip into decision-making groups through an executive's unwillingness or lack of courage to make a decision that the group may disapprove.

That the misuse and wastes involved in group activities should be watched can hardly be denied.

17. *Does he make sure that committee or group meetings are preceded by proper agenda, information gathering, analyses, and concrete proposals?* (Pp. 400–404.)

To avoid the wastes of those group meetings and committees that are necessary for effective advice, deliberation, or decision making, there are certain simple guidelines. This checkpoint summarizes one of the most important.

18. *Does he distinguish in his operations between lines of authority and lines of information?* (P. 408.)

One of the weaknesses of organization operation in practice derives from failure to distinguish between lines of authority for decision making and lines of information. The lines of authority shown on an organization chart were never meant to reflect all the lines and sources of information. They chart lines of authority for decision making. Actually a manager should be encouraged to get information directly from where it is and disregard lines of command. The only exceptions to this principle are: (1) cases where authenticated information vouched for by the manager in charge of a department is desired; (2) cases where the furnishing of information would be so time-consuming and costly as to interfere with the operations of another department manager; and (3) cases where the information may properly be classified as confidential.

If these principles are followed, much of the waste and frustration of the so-called chain of command and complicated organization structure can be avoided.

19. *Does he plan his organization structure so that he can select and develop individuals who can meet future position requirements?* (Pp. 412–417.)

For those persons in managerial positions who have some control over the form of an organization structure, one of the keys to good management is organization planning. In other words, only in seeing, as well as possible, the future shape of the structure can a manager appreciate the number and kind of managerial personnel he will need in the future. While this is difficult to do and ideally should be done for a period in the future necessary to foresee needs in time, it is an area where many errors are made.

Too many managers, at all levels, select, promote, and train people only for today's positions. The result is often that five or ten years down the road a company has a vice-president who can no longer fill the job. We are then often faced with discharging or putting on the shelf a loyal and intelligent associate who has not, and had thought been given at the time of his selection, could not have been expected to have, grown with the job.

Another major weakness from lack of organization planning is the resultant lack of making provision for development of people for future key positions. In a smaller company this may not be possible and the filling of these key positions must be handled by raiding from the outside. But for larger companies, planned development is surely the better course.

Appraising Managers as Managers: Staffing

As noted in the introduction to organizing, staffing has to do with the selection, promotion, appraisal, training, and compensation of subordinates. Since our interest is primarily in managers, many of the key checkpoints will be devoted to those who have managers as subordinates.

1. *Does he take full responsibility for the staffing of his department, even though he obtains needed assistance from the personnel department?* (Pp. 442–445.)

This is, of course, the essence of the managerial staffing function. It is emphasized because so many managers neglect taking real responsibility for it.

2. *Does he make it clear to his subordinates that every posi-tion in his department is open to the best qualified individual, either inside or outside the company?* (Pp. 448–451.)

Unless a manager is bound by a strict promotion-from-within policy imposed by his company, this should be his guide to action. An open competition policy is the only honest and viable policy a company can have. Almost all so-called promotion-from-within policies state that all positions will be filled from within and then, usually in fine print, "so long as a qualified person can be found within the company." This is bound to cause discontent and disillusionment when a com-pany does go outside, or a stagnant situation of playing it safe is tolerated so that a person can move up when his superior is promoted, dies, or retires.[4]

Under an open competition policy, a company is under real compulsion to make sure that people in the company are fairly and adequately evaluated, considered for openings, and given every possible opportunity for development. Needless to say, all these things are consistent with good managing.

3. *Does he take steps to make certain that his subordinates are given the opportunity for training for better positions, both in his operations and elsewhere in the company?* (Pp. 442–453, 508–515.)

4. *Does he utilize appropriate methods of training and developing his subordinates?* (Pp. 507–515.)

5. *Does he effectively practice coaching of subordinates as a means of training?* (Pp. 524–526.)

All three of the above checkpoints have to do with one of an executive's most important tasks—the development of those who report to him. They indicate several things. With or without the help and encouragement of the personnel de-

---

[4] As it was formerly said of the railroad industry, "When a president retires, we hire a new office boy."

partment, does he see that his subordinates are given opportunities for their own development? Another question is designed to emphasize the fact that there are many ways to help
a person in his development; too many superiors are likely to
think only of formal courses or conferences and overlook the
many other approaches to development. One question makes
a special point of coaching. Virtually everyone who has
studied management development has concluded that patient
teaching and counseling by the superior, accompanied by
appropriate delegation of authority, represent the most effective of all management development approaches. Yet it is a
rare manager who either can do it well or takes the time and
effort to do so.

Implied, but not specifically stated in question 3, is another
aspect of staffing that really borders on and could be regarded
as a phase of leadership. The intelligent manager will always
regard his subordinates as available for promotion to a better
position, whether in or out of his department and regardless
of the fact that it might be inconvenient to lose a competent
deputy. To do otherwise is to thwart a person's growth and
opportunity. Good men understandably avoid bosses who
stand in their way.

6. *Does he tend to keep subordinates who have questionable ability in their jobs?*

One of the weaknesses of many managers is their hesitation
to remove incompetent persons from their positions. Almost
all superiors have a special interest in those who report to
them and are likely to be unwilling to take action on the basis
that "Joe is a good guy," or "He has a tough job," or "He has
had a lot of bad luck lately." After taking into account the
areas a subordinate can do well in, if any, and attempting to
take advantage of these strengths, and after objective appraisal and attempts to help a man develop, there can normally be no alternative but to replace a man who cannot

perform adequately. The effective manager does this, usually recommending generous severance arrangements for a loyal person who cannot be placed in a suitable job elsewhere in the company.

7. *How well is he echeloned in his position?*

A common weakness among managers is not to have able persons in the group reporting to them. This may be due to poor development, it may be due to poor selection, it may be due to not hiring "high" enough, and it may come from the conscious or unconscious fear by a superior of having subordinates who will threaten his standing or position.

Whatever the reason, inadequate echeloning should be a matter of concern and a subject for investigation.

8. *Does he appraise his subordinates objectively and regularly on the basis of performance against preselected goals?* (Pp. 484–501.)

9. *Does he appraise his subordinates objectively and regularly on their ability to manage effectively?* (Pp. 718–724.)

10. *Does he use appraisals as a means of helping his subordinates improve their performance?* (Pp. 487–488.)

The above three questions represent checkpoints that are the subject of this book. Clearly, the discriminating and perceptive evaluating of subordinates is an important area on which to rate a manager. Also, one of the major reasons for having effective appraisal of performance against goals and of performance as a manager is to help individuals improve in each area. The superior who does not do this has not done his job.

11. *Does he select or recommend promotion of his subordinates on the basis of his objective appraisal of their performance and in the light of their potential for growth in the company?* (Pp. 484–501.)

Some would argue that appraisal should not be related to selection or promotion on the grounds that many superiors will decide what they want to do first and then make the appraisal fit the case. This is possible, but it should be avoided in other ways. It seems fairly ridiculous not to make appraisal a major basis for appointments and promotions and to do so openly. This checkpoint also requires more than judgment as to how well a man has been doing. It demands also a conscious judgment, as subject to error as this may be, of the subject's potential for growth in the company.

These are some of the most serious decisions a manager makes, and rating on them should be given a great deal of attention. If this were realized and practiced, we might avoid the many illogical instances where a man may be highly rated for several years and then have a superior recommend his discharge for incompetency!

12. *Does he take such steps and make such recommendations as he can to provide adequate and motivating compensation and conditions of work for his subordinates?* (Pp. 454–456.)

One of the keys to effective managing is having the principal do what is in his power to place his subordinates in a motivating work environment. This, of course, includes compensation, whether salary, bonuses, stock options, or other elements of pay. Naturally, a manager may be limited as to what he can do by the need for company consistency or by company policy. He may not even have the power to make the decision. But where compensation or other elements of the work environment are below par, every manager has an obligation to plead his subordinates' cases. There is probably nothing that will put more zeal and enthusiasm in a subordinate than knowing that his boss is concerned with, and working to improve, his welfare.

Appraising Managers as Managers: Directing

The managerial function of directing encompasses leading, motivating, and supervising of subordinates. It is preeminently the interpersonal part of the manager's task and requires skills and attitudes that are exceedingly difficult to measure. This is perhaps the most subjective portion of appraisal of managers as managers. However, it is hoped that, with some questions raised on key points of this function, an acceptable degree of objective appraisal can result.

1. *Does he understand what motivates his subordinates and attempt to build into their position and position environment a situation to which these motivations will respond?* (Pp. 566–588.)

While no one in his right mind would expect a manager to be an accomplished psychiatrist and no implication is intended in this question that a manager's task is to manipulate those who report to him, it is believed that any manager should understand the rudiments of the things to which people respond. For example, Maslow's hierarchy of needs— survival; safety; security, social and affiliative; ego-satisfaction and self-esteem; autonomy and independence; and self-actualization—can be readily understood and built into the environment of work. Many managers do it well, although a few seem to forget that all human beings respond to a major extent to the same sources of motivation.

2. *Does he so lead and guide his subordinates and interpret company and departmental objectives as to make them see that their own self-interest is in harmony with, although not necessarily the same as, the company's or department's goals?* (Pp. 554–555.)

This question goes to the core of direction and leadership. Obviously people have personal goals that are different from those of the company they work for. People do not live and die for old XYZ Company, but for themselves. But it is possible for the capable leader to get people to see that their own self-interest can be advanced by serving the objectives of a company or one of its departments. It is thus possible to harmonize individual and group objectives, and the good manager can and will do it. Moreover, it should never be forgotten that the essence of leadership is followership and people tend to follow those in whom they see a means of satisfying their own personal desires.

3. *Does he issue instructions that are clear, within his authority, and fully understandable to his subordinates?* (Pp. 557–560, 590–610.)

4. *Does he use effective and efficient communications techniques in dealing with subordinates?* (Pp. 590–610.)

5. *Does he engage in an appropriate amount of face-to-face contact?* (Pp. 250–251.)

As can be seen, the above three questions deal with the immensely difficult area of communication. Some prominent executives believe that this is the most important area of management. It is probably true that attaining an environment of clarity is one of the most difficult things to accomplish without spelling things out in too much detail and removing discretion and opportunity for creative work in a person's role.

Some of the communications difficulties encountered in practice are not, however, a matter of communications techniques. The author has seen many cases where communication failed because the superior did not have anything to say (usually a lack of planning) or did not know with whom to communicate on what (a matter of clear organization). But the entire subject of communications is a difficult one and the astute superior will watch for symptoms of poor communication and attempt, through help and development, to improve it.

Question 5 is aimed at assessing the appropriate amount of face-to-face communications. One exceptionally intelligent production manager attempted to run his manufacturing operations from the remote control of an array of charts and reports in his office. As good as these were, he failed as a manager primarily because he lost touch with his superintendents, his supervisors, and his workmen. People do want to see their boss and occasionally those on up the line in management. In addition, there are often matters—especially delicate ones—that cannot be handled without face-to-face contact. Also, face-to-face contact can often transmit information that no written report or graph could possibly convey. On the other hand, there are managers who do far too much of their communication on a face-to-face basis. This can be wasteful of time and may even be disruptive to those under them.

6. *Does he create an environment where people are encouraged to suggest innovation in product, process, marketing, or other company policy and planning areas?*

7. *Is he receptive to innovative ideas, suggestions, and the desire to be heard, whether from his superiors, his equals, or his subordinates?*

8. *Does he expect his subordinates to suggest changes or express objections to what they may regard as the wrong objectives, policies, and programs, or does he expect blind compliance with company policies and programs and his own decisions?*

The above three check questions reflect aspects of directing important to the development of an environment of innovativeness, free flow of ideas, and bringing into action the countless good ideas and pieces of information that now lie buried in far too many enterprises. They also emphasize the point that most people do have ideas, want to be heard and make suggestions, and chafe under one-way communication. Yet none of these questions is intended to imply that suggestions or criticism go on forever. At some time, someone must decide *a* course of action. People do expect this and will likely fume more under the indecisive weak boss than under an autocrat. Moreover, after they have had a chance to offer their ideas, to get in their "two cents' worth," most people are happy to follow a decision even if it is not what they desire.

9. *Can his subordinates reach him readily to discuss their problems and obtain guidance?*

Many managers understandably become so preoccupied with their own problems and with their many necessary contacts with associates, superiors, customers, and others that they may neglect their subordinates. The essence of direction and leadership is interpersonal relations with subordinates and this must be maintained at all costs. However, necessary and fruitful contacts can be made so as not to require too much of a time burden on a superior. There are many ways to accomplish this, one of the major being the effective application of a program of management by objectives.

10. *Does he help his subordinates to become oriented to the company's programs, objectives, and environment?*

As pointed out above in the discussion of elements in management planning, no manager can do an effective job of planning in his area unless he understands company and department objectives, policies, and the environment in which his planned operations are expected to take place. To assure this understanding is one of the major tasks of directing.

11. *Does he exercise participative leadership when useful and authoritative direction when necessary?* (Pp. 627–629.)

With emphasis on people and human relationships, and on working with people, there is a danger that a manager may make the mistake of assuming that all of his managing must be consultative or participative. In this case, he may waste time and become too indecisive. There are times when a participative approach will not work. Where the manager is the only one who possesses information, such as on upper-level decisions or policy, it would be foolish to ask his subordinates' suggestions on what he should do. There are times, too, when discussion must cease, a decision be made, and action be started. There are other times when a course of action must be followed regardless of people's feelings or suggestions. The effective manager, then, must possess a sense of knowing when to be authoritative and when to be consultative or even permissive, and how and when to blend and choose these techniques.

12. *Is he effective as a leader ("the capacity and will to rally men and women to a common purpose")?* (Pp. 612–619.)

The dominant factor in directing, and indeed in managing, is the capacity for exercising leadership. As noted above, the essence of leadership is the ability to detect what people want and to take actions that cause them to believe that, through their superior's actions, their own self-interest will be served. To a major extent people are likely to follow in an organized enterprise: (1) when they know what is expected of them — the job of planning; (2) when they have a clear role and know others' roles — the job of organizing; (3) when they are well selected, appraised, trained, and compensated — the task of staffing; (4) when they are patiently guided and helped — the task of directing; and (5) when they know how well they are doing and are given an opportunity to correct their errors — the job of controlling.

Appraising Managers as Managers: Controlling

The managerial function of control involves measuring and correcting actions to assure that plans are actually being achieved. It is the means by which the loop is closed in managing. It is singularly dependent on plans since there is no possible way a person can know whether he is going where he wants to go—the job of control—unless some planning was done by someone to show where it was intended he go.

Control in practice is largely a matter of techniques, of measures and ways of detecting deviations and taking action. But it is also a matter of simple cybernetic theory. The following diagram outlines the essence of control:

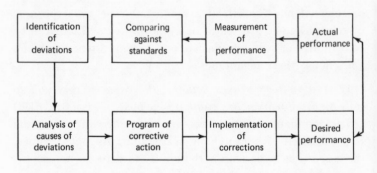

Several things can be seen from the above diagram. The time it takes to translate measurements into corrective action means that any truly successful approach to control will require means of anticipating deviations before they occur. Even the fastest possible information processing will not be fast enough. Mere observation of the steps in the loop will disclose a number of difficulties in effective control and a number of time-consuming actions. It also shows the importance of standards—criteria of performance to be measured—and of carefully choosing them since a manager cannot watch everything.

1. *How effectively does he tailor his control techniques and standards to reflect his plans?* (Pp. 639–644.)

Since every plan differs from another, either in a minor or a major way, the effective manager will tailor his controls and select critical standards so that he can watch the performance of planning programs for which he has a responsibility.

2. *Does he use control techniques, where possible, to anticipate deviations in plans?* (Pp. 644, 647–648.)

As pointed out above, because analysis of deviations from plans and development and implementation of corrections take time, the ideal control system must be forward looking. There are rather few devices available that do this, such as various kinds of forecasting, particularly cash forecasting, and utilization of planning networks (PERT/CPM). Until management techniques in this area are improved, one cannot expect much. But an appraiser can expect awareness of the problem and some attempt to anticipate deviations.

3. *Do his control techniques and information promptly report deviations from plans?* (P. 644.)

Although accurate anticipation cannot often be expected, the least that can be expected is that the manager develop control techniques and information sources that will give him the most prompt possible reporting of deviations.

4. *Does he develop and rely on objective or verifiable control information?* (P. 645.)

Control information should be as objective and as verifiable as possible for two very important reasons. In the first place, if it is not, the manager may not be sure that deviations have really taken place. Secondly, his subordinate is likely not to believe that the error is real and may become defensive, with the result that he may not take action.

5. *Does he develop controls that point up exceptions at critical points?* (Pp. 644–645.)

The time-honored exception principle is not enough. The important thing is that a manager should look not only at exceptions to planned performance, but also at exceptions at critical, important points, points that make the most difference in the success of a program.

6. *Are his control techniques and information designed to show exactly where in the organization deviations occur?* (P. 646.)

It is not enough to know that something is going awry. One must know where in the structure of organization the deviation is taking place, which manager is responsible for the errant action. Indeed, if a superior does not know who is responsible and where, it is almost better that he not know at all since there is rather little he can do about it.

The proper discharge of control depends in large part on clear organization. It likewise depends on designing the flow of control information to reflect organization structure. This is often the problem in some cost accounting. It may tell the manager that a product is costing more than was planned, but it may not show who is responsible for the costs being out of line.

7. *Are his control techniques and information understandable to those who must take action?* (P. 647.)

What a man cannot understand or will not understand, and it really does not matter much which, he will not use. So many of the data ground out today with automatic data processing are not adequately designed to serve the needs of managers and are often not presented in a form they can or will understand. Much of this output, then, has questionable value for control.

8. *Does he take prompt action when unplanned variations in performance occur?* (Pp. 644, 647–648.)

Control must mean action. It does no good for a manager to have tailored information telling him at critical points that a planned performance is going astray. The significant thing is whether or not he delays, watches the problem grow, or takes prompt action to correct deviations.

9. *When deviations from subordinates' plans occur, does he help them take action?*

While it is not intended to imply by this checkpoint that a manager will step in and take over his subordinate's job and put out fires, there is every reason to believe and expect that the effective manager will do what he can to help his subordinate. After all, if the subordinate fails, he may also plunge his boss into failure.

10. *Does he operate effectively under variable (budget) profit and performance plans?* (Pp. 655–659.)

There is no operation too small or simple, or too large and complex, to operate under a form of variable budget or profit plan. This is a system in which all expenses at every location of expense responsibility are divided between those that vary with volume of operation and those that are variable only with time. Under this system it is possible to plan in advance what expenses *should* be at various volume levels. The question, then, is whether the manager being appraised understands the system and operates effectively within it. Even in enterprises where the total operation does not for some reason operate under variable budgets, there is nothing to stop an individual manager from utilizing, as best he can, a system for himself. Indeed, he should do so.

11. *Does he supplement his (budget) profit and perfor-mance plans with other devices of control?* (Pp. 659–662, 664–691.)

As good for planning and control as budgets or profit plans are, a manager should be appraised on how and to what extent he utilizes the many other devices of control which are avilable and are being developed.

12. *Does he recognize and implement the network nature of his planning and control problems?* (Pp. 681–686.)

As emphasized in the discussion of planning, effective plans almost invariably represent a network. In other words, plans seldom operate linearly, but rather one project goes on while another is being accomplished although they have critical interdependencies. The same phenomena must be recognized with control. Checking on whether a given program is progressing as planned must include recognition of its interrelationship with other projects. Particularly if one plan is late or exceeding costs, this can have an effect on what happens to other plans of which it is a part or a prerequisite. In control, as in planning, the effective manager makes a habit of seeing not only whether one program is slipping, but also what the effect is on a given system of interlocking programs.

13. *Does he keep abreast of, and utilize, newer techniques of planning and control?* (Pp. 664–691.)

Perhaps more progress has been made in recent years in techniques of planning and control than in any other area of management. The various systems approaches, operations research and simulation, PERT/CPM, direct costing, and variable budgeting are among these newer techniques. A manager can hardly be regarded as doing his job well unless he keeps abreast of these newer techniques, understands their basic nature, and applies them appropriately in his work.

14. *Does he develop and utilize overall methods of control of performance, where suitable, in his operations?* (Pp. 694–712.)

Most control devices are, in a sense, partial controls. They measure specific actions and plans. But what a manager should be interested in is whether the *total* results for which he is responsible are what are desired. In the operation of an integrated division, for example, the manager will utilize such measures as total profit or loss, or rate of return on investment. In an engineering project, he will be interested in a control approach that will measure how the total project is succeeding by way of product quality, costs, and schedule. Clearly, overall controls are especially applicable to the manager who is at a level and in a position to be responsible for some integrated result rather than only a part of a program.

15. *Does he help his subordinates develop control techniques and information that will show them how well they are doing in order to assist in "control by self-control"?*

As Peter Drucker so aptly said many years ago, "The best kind of control is control by self-control." In other words, if the manager concerned knows the objectives he is expected to achieve and the plans he is responsible for accomplishing, and if he has the right kind of information that tells *him* how well *he* is doing, he will in most cases undertake corrections himself rather than wait for his boss to detect deviations and require corrections. But if control by self-control is to succeed, people require help from their superior. This help may come in the form of guidance in the design of suitable techniques, assistance in obtaining information needed, or in other ways.

16. *Does he keep his superior informed of significant (to his superior) problems and errors in his operation, their causes, and steps being taken to correct them?*

This standard for effective management may be summarized in the statement that no superior wants to be surprised on matters of importance. The superior is, after all, responsible for the successful performance of those who report to him. When a subordinate manager has a problem or sees a deviation from plans developing that may affect his superior's responsibility, he must disclose it immediately to his boss, along with the program for correction he is implementing. In one of the large aerospace companies, a division manager found himself seriously overrun in expenses and behind schedule on a major project. Yet the surprised and enraged head of the company did not know of the trouble until a top Department of Defense official walked in his office ready to cancel the contract. Problem watchers, or those who see a problem developing but hope that it will go away, can never be successful managers. Since a superior may miss some of these developing errors, even though admittedly if his control techniques and information are adequate he probably should not, those responsible to him must keep him informed of significant deviations.

Developing Ratings on Each Checklist Item

In developing the above checklist of items against which effectiveness of managing, as managing, might be assessed, it was hoped, as pointed out earlier, to make each a "go" or "no-go" judgment and thereby introduce a high degree of objectivity. But this has been found to be impracticable and resort had to be made to qualitative judgments on each item. In order to give these qualitative judgments some rigor, however, the following scale and definitions have been used (note: to avoid too much meaningless arithmetic, only two ratings for most steps are suggested).

5.0   *Superior:* a standard of performance which could not be improved upon under any circumstances or conditions known to the rater.

4.0 or 4.5   *Excellent:* a standard of performance which leaves little of any consequence to be desired.

3.0 or 3.5   *Good:* a standard of performance above the average and meeting all normal requirements of the position.

2.0 or 2.5   *Average:* a standard of performance regarded as average for the position involved and the people available.

1.0 or 1.5   *Fair:* a standard of performance below the normal requirements of the position but one that may be regarded as marginally or temporarily acceptable.

0.0   *Inadequate:* a standard of performance regarded as unacceptable for the position involved.

X   *Not Applicable to the Position:* There may be certain standards that are not applicable to a position or of so little importance in operation as not to deserve a rating.

N   *Do Not Know Accurately Enough for Rating:* It would not be expected that every manager would know enough about a subordinate's performance to rate every item on the checklist; since no judgment should be made from ignorance, an *N* rating is entirely appropriate on any given item. However, it is assumed that the superior will watch in the future for evidence on these items.

In averaging ratings for any area, only the questions rated should be averaged, excluding the not applicable questions

(X) and those on which the rater has inadequate information (N). As implied above, managers should not be discouraged from using these X and N ratings. The system should only be applied to those items applicable to a given job and to those on which the rater has enough knowledge to rate. However, because the checklist items are generally applicable to managing positions and because, as raters gain experience in applying the system, they will tend increasingly to watch for evidence on each item, the number of unrated questions will tend to be few.

chapter six

Appraisal of Managers
as Managers:
Operating the Program

In operating the program of appraisal of managers as managers outlined in the previous chapter, there are a number of practical suggestions that can be made. Also, clinical experience with the program for five years in a multinational company has disclosed certain advantages and difficulties which will be discussed here. While the program is admittedly still experimental and should be regarded as such, suggestions can be offered for making it effective in practice.

How to Operate the Program

As is readily apparent, this program applies only to the rating of individuals in a managerial position, that is, those who have people reporting to them. Because it attempts to use the fundamentals of management as standards, it is applicable to all levels of managing, from chief executive to first-line supervision. However, as will be appreciated, certain checkpoints will be more important in upper than in lower levels. For example, a lower-level supervisor may not be involved in making functional authority delegations (question 13 in Organizing), or the utilization of overall methods of control may not be applicable in his job (question 14 in Controlling). Likewise, for first-line supervisors, those questions which imply that the subordinate is also a manager may not apply (see, for example, in Planning, questions 3, 4, 5 and in Organizing, questions dealing with delegation). Thus raters should be warned to exclude and mark with an *X* those questions not applicable to a given position. Averages would, of course, be computed on those applicable questions answered and those on which a rater has enough information to answer.

The Rating Process Experience has indicated that formal rating should be done twice annually for the best results. In this, the superior rates his subordinate manager on all applicable questions of the checklist on which he has knowledge, adhering as strictly as possible to the standards applied for the numerical ratings. It is also good practice to have the person being evaluated rate himself. Then the superior and subordinate go over the ratings together, item by item. The obvious advantages of doing this are obtaining mutual understanding of ratings, the opportunity to give evidence of weaknesses and strengths of the manager being rated, and, above all, the use of appraisal as a learning process.

It should further be understood that the degree of discrimination and objectivity in rating ought to be used by a rater's superior as an element in his appraisal of the rater. To assure some feel of this quality as well as to assure that the rater is handling his ratings competently, it is urged that a superior's rating of his subordinate be reviewed by the superior's superior and that this review be made a part of the record. Such review can be handled by the superior's superior through rating the former's subordinate on all the questions, or more likely by a summary review of the extent of agreement or disagreement.

Use of a Standard for Concepts   Because management concepts are by no means subject to common understanding by those engaged in practice, and often this semantics "jungle" leads to wide misunderstanding among managers in an enterprise, it is essential that some standard management book be used as a point of reference for clarification of terms, concepts, and the meaning of techniques and approaches. In this book, after each checklist question where there might possibly be any misunderstanding, page references are given to the widely used management book of which the writer is co-author.[1] But any of the other commonly accepted standard management books could be used.[2]

The Question of Weighting   Questions have been raised as to whether the individual checklist questions under each managerial function should be weighted. It is true that, in most operations, certain items are more important than others.

[1] H. Koontz and C. O'Donnell, *Principles of Management,* 4th ed. (New York: McGraw-Hill Book Company, 1968).

[2] Most of the terms and concepts are dealt with competently in the following standard management books, among others: H. H. Albers, *Principles of Organization and Management,* 2d ed. (New York: John Wiley & Sons, Inc., 1965); E. Dale, *Management: Theory and Practice,* 2d ed. (New York: Mc Graw-Hill Book Company, 1969); J. G. Longenecker, *Principles of Management and Organizational Behavior,* 2d ed. (Columbus, Ohio: Charles E. Merrill Books, Inc., 1969); D. E. McFarland, *Management Principles and Practices* (New York: The Macmillan Company, 1958); F. G. Moore, *Management: Organization and Practice* (New York: Harper & Row, Publishers, Incorporated, 1964); W. H. Newman, *Administrative Action,* 2d ed. (Englewood Cliffs, N.J.: Prentice-Hall, Inc., 1961); W. H. Newman and C. E. Summer, Jr., *The Process of Management* (Englewood Cliffs, N.J.: Prentice-Hall, Inc., 1961); G. R. Terry, *Principles of Management,* 5th ed. (Homewood, Ill.: Richard D. Irwin, Inc., 1968).

For example, delegation by results expected is the most important single principle of delegation; the issuance of clear instructions is less important in the area of directing than creating an environment for performance and innovation; or recognizing and implementing the network nature of planning and control problems, included in Controlling, may be somewhat less significant than other control questions.

It is possible that the questions could be weighted. However, this appears to introduce an element of complexity not justified by the extensiveness of the checklist items. Furthermore, in reviewing these items, there is real question as to whether many of the individual items are really of greatly different importance. In a very real sense, they represent links in a chain, and failure in one or two can mean deficiency in the total quality of managing. Moreover, this is, at best, a rather crude tool and there would appear to be little advantage in attempting to platinum-plate it.

The Summary Report If the appraisal of managers as managers is to be used as a basis for appraising an individual (along with appraisal of his performance in setting and meeting preselected objectives) for purposes of development, promotion, or compensation, as the author thinks it should, the total appraisal of performance as a manager should be summarized periodically.

To do this, a summary report might include a statement showing the average ratings for each managerial function, accompanied by a narrative under each by both the superior of the person being rated and the superior's superior as to the significant strengths and weaknesses of the subordinate being rated in each managerial area. Over time, too, previous average ratings in each function should be shown on the summary report. Such a sample summary report form is shown in Appendix 3 and sample reports in Appendix 4.

Because the intent of any appraisal should be to be constructive, the best results will be obtained by having the manager doing the rating indicate on the summary what action he has taken, or intends to take, by training or otherwise, to improve deficiencies. Especially when this is done, experience has shown that both raters and ratees find the system to be a pleasant management development exercise rather than an unpleasant task of standing in judgment on another person.

Advantages of the Program

In the years of experience with the program, certain advantages have clearly emerged. These include both those expected and designed into the system and one, at least, that was disclosed only in practice.

Focus on the Essentials of Managing   As intended, and unlike other approaches to evaluating managers, this system of evaluation does focus on the essentials of managing. As crude as the principles and the entire science of management may be, there are many principles that give an indication of what makes for effective managing. An attempt has been made in the checklist items to incorporate, in question form, those that do give guidance to effective managing, as managing. By doing so, at least those in a managerial role are being judged on their *managerial* ability and practice.

The advantage of thus breaking down the fundamentals of management is to give some meaning, in fairly specific terms, to what management really is. As one top manager declared to the author, "How can you talk of management development and appraisal when all most people can say is that managing is getting things done through people or is planning, organizing, staffing, directing, and controlling?" He was right. This does not explain managing. One must go to a much more comprehensive summary of the basics of management.

The clarifying and developmental aspect of this appraisal was shown in the early clinical experience with the program. When the company involved agreed to adopt a total program of appraising managers against objectives and as managers, and to tie these appraisals to its bonus and promotion program, the chief executive with whom the author had long worked insisted that he be the first person evaluated and that the author do it! The executive appraised himself and the author appraised him (somewhat reluctantly). Despite the author adopting an objective and hard stance in his appraisal, he found that the executive had been even tougher on himself. The encouraging thing, however, was that, after the appraisal review and going over each item of the checklist, the chief executive (who was actually a very good manager) responded, "I have taken classes and seminars on management and I have read books on the subject, *even* your book; but this is the first time I have ever understood what managing is all about!"

Communications and Semantics   One of the unexpected benefits of the program was how much it improved management communications throughout the company, both in the United States and overseas, through developing a common understanding of management terms and concepts. "Line" and "staff," both generally misunderstood terms, now came into common use and meaning. The concepts of "verifiable objectives," "flexibility," "policy," "delegation," and "variable budgets" took on uniform meaning throughout the company.

Likewise, many management techniques became uniformly understood. Mystery all but disappeared from the process of goal setting and developing a network of goals, greater care was displayed in establishing and disseminating planning premises, and efforts were made to avoid the entanglements of delegating functional authority. A manager's responsibility for staffing became more thoroughly understood and followed. The process of appraisal itself was undertaken with greater care and without the reluctance encountered with earlier traditional methods. Considerable inventiveness came to be displayed in the development and application of management controls.

These and other advantages of clarification in an area which is often unclear arose, of course, from two major factors. In the first place, on a worldwide basis, the company used a common source for the meaning of management terms and techniques. In the second place, by having the appraisal system applied in a way that emphasized these things, the environment tended to force managers to be sure that they did understand.

A Tool for Management Development   The very rating process itself, by focusing on the basics of management and their application in practice, became a powerful tool for management development. We are all the same. We can do things wrong for years without intending to and without knowing. But when our errors can be called to our attention in a definite and fairly objective way, we learn and learn quickly. Also, there are many aspects of managing that may have escaped even the astute manager's attention. The importance and nature of verifiable goals, planning premises, utilization of the critical factor in decision making, distinction between lines of authority and lines of information, judicious use of participative and authoritative leadership, and the design of tailored controls can be easily overlooked unless there is some means of bringing these forcibly to the attention of the practicing manager.

In addition, the whole system of appraisal, including setting of goals and achieving them, can become a useful means of guiding management development. There is, understandably, much waste in sending a manager to programs where much that is taught is what he already knows, in the hope that some things will be taught that he did not already know. The system of appraisal offered here does help to identify the areas where weaknesses exist and should make it possible to aim development to these. Moreover, as a superior develops effectiveness as an appraiser, he also becomes a better coach as to what is effective management practice. The process of evaluation and comparing notes with his subordinates gives him the platform for practical coaching.

Acts as a Check on Performance against Goals   One of the advantages of supplementing appraisal of effectiveness in attaining preselected goals with an appraisal of managers as managers is the fact that the latter acts as a check on the former. If a manager has an outstanding performance in meeting or surpassing objectives and yet is shown to be a less than average manager, those in charge should look for the reason. Normally, one would expect a truly effective manager to be also effective in meeting goals.

In the operation of this program, there have been instances where goal performance and managerial performance did not agree. In one case, the manager of a divisional operation with responsibility for marketing and manufacturing was given a poor rating as a manager. Yet his operation far surpassed the sales and profit goals that had been set. Investigation showed two factors that tended to explain this inconsistency. The major one was that he was in a market which had suddenly expanded and almost anyone could have made an outstanding sales and profit performance. Another factor was that his second-in-command was found to be the real, imaginative operating head of the operation, had taken the reins from his boss, and was actually responsible for much of the performance.

A Tool for Improving Managing   The main purpose of the program of appraisal of managers as managers is to improve the quality of managing in a company. Periodic evaluation of a person as a manager serves to remind both the supervisor and his subordinate of their true function. It is always easy to get so involved with day-to-day problems and activities that one forgets about the entire task of managing. Like a pilot, a manager needs a kind of checklist of the major activities involved in managing. He needs also some means of forcing him to consider and weigh the elements in this checklist. The time spent in thinking about these things and being required to appraise performance should go far toward improving the quality of managing.

In the clinical test of this program, the worldwide improvement of the quality of managing was significant, and the growth in sales and profits of the company was considerable. While other factors undoubtedly contributed to the company's performance, there can be no doubt that more sophisticated and able management had a significant impact.

This is as it should be. There are few, if any, today who would doubt that the quality of managing is a critical factor in the success of any enterprise, business or otherwise. Obviously any technique, imperfect as it may be, that will contribute to managerial effectiveness should make a difference in performance.

Difficulties with the Program

Experience with the program in actual operation disclosed a number of problems and difficulties. Anyone contemplating using it or any modification of it should profit by being aware of these.

Need for Separate Checklist for Nonmanagerial Positions   One of the problems encountered has been that the proposed checklist only applies to managerial positions, or the managerial aspects of positions that are both managerial and staff in nature. Admittedly, many positions have both managerial and staff elements in them. A chief engineer, for example, is head of the engineering department and usually also the primary engineering adviser of the company. Likewise, a personnel manager, a controller, or even the head of marketing will likely be both a manager of his department and the staff specialist in his area.

The question has been raised as to how nonmanagerial activities may be evaluated. This is a shortcoming of the program. First, it is intended to apply only to managerial positions. While there are elements of staff behavior that could probably be put in a checklist, based on the fundamentals of management, this appraisal program does not do it. Also, perhaps the best way of measuring the effectiveness of staff operations, even in positions that are also managerial, is through setting verifiable objectives for this advisory function. This can and should be done.

Tendency for Checkpoints to Proliferate   There is a tendency in practice for the number of checkpoints to proliferate. As experience develops, there are always elements of managing that seem to call for special attention. In the clinical history of the project this occurred. The program started out with a total of eighty-seven checkpoints covering the five functions and grew to ninety-nine, before it was cut back to the present total of seventy-three.

Those that were added and dropped were important but were found to be incorporated, or could be covered, in other checkpoints. For example, one—"Does he teach the meaning of company policies to his subordinates?"—was believed to be incorporated in the question of whether the manager understands the role of company policies and assures that his subordinates do likewise. Others, like "Does he make sure not to have unnecessary line assistants?" or "Does he exercise care not to regard delegation of authority as insulation?" were felt to be covered by other questions or to be of relatively minor importance.

The main purpose is to keep the checklist points to a minimum to avoid making overly complex a program that, at best, seems fairly complicated. The guideline followed was that the list must consist of as few items as possible, but enough to highlight in each functional area the basics of managing to make sure that the manager was not overlooking anything of strategic importance.

Belief That the System Is Too Complex One of the major problems encountered in practice was the belief by some that the system was too complex. A list of seventy-three checkpoints, even though spread over five basic functions of managers, does appear to be involved. There may even be objections that this requires too much time for the superior to think through and rate his subordinates. It does require some time. But a few hours each six months, plus a few hours to sit down and discuss the ratings with a subordinate, seem to be a very small price indeed to pay for appraising the managerial effectiveness of a subordinate. There is probably not much of greater importance for a superior to do. And when the opportunities for coaching and development are considered, this is an exceptionally small price to pay if the result is any improvement at all in the quality of managing.

The Problem of Subjectivity The program still suffers from the fact that ratings are established for each checklist item and these grades are bound to have a high degree of subjectivity involved in them. It is hoped, however, and experience has proved, that the large number of checkpoints, being specific as they are, tends to reduce the subjectivity of the overall program. An ideal program would have no subjectivity and the questions would be answerable with a yes or no. But no way has been found to eliminate completely judgment on the "how well" a man does.

In addition to the fairly large number of checkpoints, the element of subjectivity has been reduced in several other ways. One of these is establishing fairly rigorous standards for giving meaning to such grades as "excellent" and "good." Another is the recommended practice of having the superior's superior review the ratings. Actual comparing of ratings with the subordinate after his self-rating and a requirement that the summary include a narrative outlining strengths and weaknesses and giving examples are also important safeguards. In practice, too, the top management committee that reviewed and compared the appraisals and ratings detected weaknesses in the degree of subjectivity and discrimination of the raters, and these were brought to the attention of the managers involved.

Inapplicability of Certain Checklist Items in Smaller Departments   In smaller departments or in less complex operations, certain checklist items were found to be inapplicable. For example, the problem of delegating functional authority, or of developing too many levels, or planning an organization structure, among others, might not be applicable to a given position, particularly those at lower levels. These need not, of course, cause difficulties since, in the proper operation of the program, managers should not be discouraged from marking inapplicable items with an X and making the ratings depend upon those that are applicable.

Tendency for Certain Checkpoints to Lose Apparent Pertinence   One of the difficulties encountered in practice was the tendency for certain checkpoints to lose apparent pertinence. After a manager learns thoroughly the nature and use of staff, for example, he may continue to do it well. Or, as in the case of such things as setting and utilizing verifiable objectives or employing and following variable budgets, once learned, the manager will probably continue to do them very well. The result is that raters may feel there is no further need to rate these items, but rather a need to concentrate on those where deficiencies exist. This attitude was encountered after several years of experience.

But even where a manager knows certain basics and practices them well, they should not be dropped from the list. In the first place, the very repetition in rating will be the best assurance that they will continue to be done well. In the second place, there are few checkpoints where performance cannot be further improved. A third consideration is the fact that superiors and those above them may wish to compare management quality and improvement over a number of managers in the enterprise.

Making the Most Effective Use of the Program

If the above program suggested for the appraisal of managers as managers is to make the contribution to management appraisal that is hoped, those who operate it must remember several things.

Make Sure the Rationale of the Program Is Understood   As with all programs of this kind, it is imperative that people understand what it is, why it is used, and what it is intended to do. Unless those who operate under such programs understand the rationale and the philosophy, they may look on it as another gimmick or "personnel program" and treat it as such.

Should Be Used with a Program of Appraising against Objectives Although it has been made abundantly clear in this book that a program of appraising managers as managers will have less than desirable success unless it is used with a program of appraising managerial performance against preset verifiable objectives, this point should again be emphasized. What basically is desired from all managers is performance in the attainment of enterprise objectives. As has been pointed out earlier in the book, appraising only on the basis of performance against goals has certain weaknesses. If it is true, as is widely believed and as this author is convinced, that, for persons in a managerial role, the capacity to manage efficiently and effectively will make the most difference in the long run, then the quality of managing should be assessed. But managers do not operate in a vacuum. They manage to assure that group effort accomplishes desired objectives. Therefore, appraisal should be tied to both aspects of performance.

Attempt to Avoid Indiscriminate Rating One of the deficiencies of the suggested program for appraising managers as managers is the subjectivity involved in rating on each checklist item. Methods have been introduced to reduce this, there is a fairly large number of checkpoints to be rated, and it is assumed that this approach will be supplemented by appraising performance against verifiable objectives. Nonetheless the danger of indiscriminate grading still exists.

Much of this can be avoided by superiors up the line in an organization reviewing the ratings and making clear that discrimination in rating will itself be a major factor in considering a manager's competence. Much can be avoided also by having the subordinate being rated rate himself and then have his superior compare his ratings with those of the subordinate, utilizing this opportunity to bring out specific instances of strengths or weaknesses in managing.

Another means of forcing discrimination, as well as one of forcing people to take the program seriously, is to utilize the ratings for such important purposes as bonus awards or promotions. If bonus awards are tied to appraisals, for example, and if these awards are made by an independent agency, such as the bonus committee of a board of directors, the pressure for serious and accurate appraisals can be very great. Examples of such summary appraisals by a company bonus committee may be found in Appendix 5.

Subordinate Self-Rating Is Highly Desirable   Although probably not essential, as already indicated the practice of having subordinates rate themselves before the superior's rating is disclosed to them is highly desirable. This gives the subordinate a chance to consider himself in his role as a manager and forces him to look at the wider spectrum of his managerial position. It sets a far more open and constructive tone for the superior's review with his subordinate. And it tends to force the superior to be reasonably objective in his rating, or at least to look for evidence to support his rating. It likewise increases the chance that the appraisal will be a development experience.

Concepts Should Be Applied Uniformly and Clearly   One of the elements of the proposed program is to have managers use a common source of reference for the meaning of management concepts, terms, techniques, and approaches. While there is an increasing degree of commonality developing among writers of management textbooks and even among many managers, there are still considerable semantic differences. If the appraisal system suggested here is to work well, these differences must be resolved and a common semantics used at least within a company.

This means that some book on management, or, as with the St. Regis Paper Company, a company manual, should be selected as the standard and should be made available to the raters for their reference. It is not of urgent importance what book is used. It is of critical importance that persons being rated and those rating speak the same language.

Time Must Be Spent   There can be no doubt that, if this program is to contribute to more effective management, those involved must be expected to spend the time necessary to make it work. But this time is not as great as might at first be supposed. The fairly large number of checkpoints, as well as the necessity of being sure that those involved understand the terms and techniques, may seem at first sight to require a great deal of time.

It should not be forgotten that all the checkpoint questions deal with matters that a superior manager should be watching and be involved in virtually on a daily basis. He should, then, be intimately conversant with what his subordinates are doing as managers. To summarize these by reference to a checklist and rating of each item should not be a difficult separate exercise, although some time must be spent in coming to conclusions. Knowing the nature and quality of a subordinate's managerial activities is certainly not separate from a superior's job. It is his job.

Experience has shown that the time required is not excessive. While it may vary between individuals, it is believed that no more than one hour is required to rate each subordinate and an equivalent time to review the ratings with him. Assuming that a manager has seven subordinates and that he does the ratings twice a year, the time required per year to rate his subordinates on performance as a manager would be approximately twenty-eight hours; and with four managerial subordinates it would be sixteen hours in a year. Even adding time for the review by a superior of his subordinates' rating of those who report to him, the hours required are likely to be increased only some 50 percent.

While this does take a meaningful piece of a manager's time in the course of a year, it is not excessive for so important a task. If the payoff to the superior is better subordinate managers, far more than this can be saved in dealing with the errors and omissions of less qualified subordinates. Indeed, the entire task of evaluation is certainly one of the most important things a manager can do.

chapter seven

Toward More Effective
Appraisals

After many years of frustration from traditional approaches
to managerial appraisal, primarily based on evaluating traits,
there is real hope that this key aspect of managing is now
becoming meaningful. Certainly, appraisal of managerial
ability based on performance against preselected verifiable
objectives is a tremendous step in the right direction. It
is such a breakthrough, however, only if it is utilized with
intelligence. To be sure, it is a common sense approach to
appraisal, but common sense in practice is too often un-
common. It concentrates, as it should, on what a manager
does rather than upon what someone subjectively thinks of
him. When utilized as a standard for evaluation along with
appraisal of a manager as a manager, there is hope that we
are, at long last, beginning to approach the area of evaluating managers with logic and effectiveness.

But devices and approaches will not solve the problem. In fact, there is ever the danger that people will adopt the techniques without accompanying them with an understanding of the philosophy, without the tools and assistance, the hard work, time commitment, and leadership to make them work.

It has been emphasized repeatedly in this book that even the best programs fail unless the right things are done with them. No management technique or approach is self-actuating. It requires patient leadership, intelligent application, and time commitment. But in this area it should be worth it. As has been said before, there is little dispute that the quality and vigor of managers make the difference, at least in long-term success, in any enterprise, whether it is business, government, education, or other types. There should likewise be no doubt that, if we are to have competent managers in an enterprise, this cannot happen without effective selection, appraisal, development, and motivation. These are all links in the same chain, and appraisal has historically been the weakest one.

The Requirement of Managerial Time and Attention

If any improvement in managerial practice is to be achieved and the most effective kind of management assured, it stands to reason that one of the essential requirements is a commitment of managerial time and attention. Anything worthwhile in the area of managing requires time and attention, a true sense of commitment to the program, a dedicated desire to make it work. This is true at all levels, and especially from those in the position of top leadership.

The Danger of Executive Malnutrition   One of the great dangers underlying any management technique or approach is that it will die from inadequate care and feeding, particularly from top management. We have seen that happen with many good programs, from variable budgeting, PERT/CPM, and management development to managerial appraisal. In one company, for example, where management by verifiable objectives made an early start in this country and where tangibly measurable results in improved productivity and morale occurred, it is sad to relate that the program faded and became a virtually useless paper-work exercise. On investigation it was found that a new president and his major division managers had become so preoccupied in playing the conglomerate game that they ceased to give the program leadership and constant feeding. Even more, the program no longer became a primary means of determining bonuses, stock options, or promotions. Nor was it used as a key to management development. The results were predictable. A decline in interest and effectiveness occurred.

It is understandable that the demands on the time of top executives are such as to make them hope and believe that, when a given program is operating well or a problem is solved, they can go on to other problems. Every alert top executive has far more problems and opportunities than he has time to deal with them. Priorities must be assigned. However, in doing so, it seems especially foolish to lower the priority on one of the most essential elements of an enterprise operation—the maintenance and improvement of the quality of its managers.

Programs Are Not Separate from Operations When one considers the managerial time and attention required for successful operation of the programs suggested in this book, one cannot help but be impressed that they are not additional, or separate, things for a manager to do. They are a part of his job. They fit into his operations, are not separate from them.

This is particularly true with appraisal of performance against verifiable objectives. Management by objectives is a way of managing. The very essence of managing involves setting meaningful, actionable, verifiable objectives; selecting the means of reaching them; having competent people in the right positions to contribute to their attainment; and through measurement and correction, assuring that these objectives are achieved. It really does not matter whether an organization approaches management by objectives through using it for appraisal, for solving the problems of budgeting, or as a total system of managing; the operation is the same. In any case, appraisal is a resultant of what is and should be done and not a separate program.

This is not quite so apparent in the case of appraising managers as managers. But it should be. Certainly every manager, as a central part of his job, has the obligation to make sure that managerial quality for which he is responsible is of the highest possible caliber. This is not a special program imposed on top of normal duties, even though the inept traditional approaches of the past may have made appraisal seem so. By having a tool that will give fairly objective guidelines as to what good managing is and how well those in managerial roles are undertaking their job, this aspect of evaluation is certainly operational.

Time Spent May Save Time   What is often overlooked is that the time spent in doing effective managerial appraisal may actually save time. In effective programs of management by objectives, managers have universally found this to be true. The time spent in helping subordinates set objectives, in clarifying their authority and duties, in making decisions to make it possible for them to operate, and in knowing what to watch in discharging their responsibility for control has been more than made up by the time saved in dealing with problems and decisions piecemeal, in holding time-consuming meetings for "coordination," and in discovering and fixing mistakes.

Limited experience with appraisal of managers as managers has disclosed the same experience. It has long been realized that the most effective and knowledgeable managers make fewer mistakes, create fewer problems, and require less time of their superior. If the quality of management at all levels can be improved through specific coaching, understanding of what is involved in managing, and managerial development, the time spent in this program should be more than saved. There is evidence that this has occurred.

Benefits   Although specific benefits from these programs, particularly in terms of increased profits, are difficult to assess, largely because of such intervening variables as market and product innovation, there is some evidence that definite improvements do result. Raia found at the Purex Corporation an increase of productivity of 18 percent over the first few years of operation of its verifiable goals program, compared to decreasing productivity in the immediate years before.[1] Wikstrom reported a case where a division manager had prepared a budget with great care, but, after the introduction of management by objectives, his subordinates were able to set goals for profit $500,000 higher than the budget and actually accomplished 80 percent of these with a resultant increase of profits of some $400,000 above that planned for in a previously "tight" budget.[2]

Other benefits found in the few before-and-after studies that have been made include such significant improvements as increased awareness of company goals, better communi-

[1] A. P. Raia, "A Second Look at Management Goals and Controls," *California Management Review,* vol. 8, no. 4, pp. 49–58, at p. 49 (Summer, 1966).

[2] W. S. Wikstrom, *Managing by—and with—Objectives* (New York: National Industrial Conference Board, Inc., 1968), p. 15.

cations, higher morale and sense of commitment, greater satisfaction from a sense of accomplishment, better self-control, less managerial preoccupation with "fighting fires," more useful accounting reports, better organization structure, and more sophisticated planning and control.[3] These results are, indeed, impressive.

The actual benefits of appraising managers as managers are a little more difficult to measure objectively. In the first place, clinical experience has been limited. In the second place, it is difficult to isolate specific improvements that come from a better quality of managing. In the one company where the author has applied this program, there is evidence of very profitable growth and certainly of improved sophistication and ability of managers throughout the company.

The Desirability of Objectivity, Clarity, and Simplicity

Objectivity　At many points in this book, the desirability of objectivity has been underscored. This has been the major deficiency of the traditional trait-oriented evaluation approach. Lack of objectivity has led to reluctance by people to appraise, and to fairly meaningless ratings when they did appraise. Managing, being by its very nature an interpersonal activity, is naturally highly subjective. But appraisal, if it is to be useful for the many purposes it ought to be, should clearly be as objective as possible.

Appraisal of performance against preselected verifiable objectives does have a high degree of objectivity. It is not, however, completely objective. Whether the goals set have the "right" degree of stretch or pull is largely a matter of

[3] All these results are documented in the Raia and Wikstrom studies. They also agree with the author's findings in cases with which he has worked.

judgment. Often, too, the extent to which a goal is accomplished, especially a qualitative goal, has elements of subjectivity in it. Likewise, the question of whether a person succeeded or failed to meet a goal due to factors beyond his control is difficult to weigh objectively.

Moreover, as the author has readily recognized, the ratings on each checklist question in appraising managers as managers suffer from subjectivity. Some of this has been avoided by the large number of specific checkpoints, some has been reduced by attempting to apply rigorous standards to each rating, some has been dealt with by providing upper-level review, and more has been eliminated by urging narrative supplements with specific incidents.

While admitting that no system of measurement yet known eliminates subjectivity, there can be no doubt that the combination of programs recommended here is far more objective than any of the traditional appraisal systems. It could be estimated that the approach of appraising performance against verifiable objectives is some 80 percent objective and the program of appraising managers as managers may be 60 percent objective. This is a quantum jump from former systems which were almost completely subjective.

Clarity One of the major problems in management is clarity. Observation of management practice over many years shows strikingly how many difficulties are caused by the widespread existence of misunderstanding. In a way, this should not be surprising. Management is, as yet, a highly inexact science dealing with an immensely complex set of variables, both inside and outside the enterprise, of which the variables of people's psychological and sociological behavior patterns are perhaps the most complex.

This being so, continuing efforts must be made to clarify any useful management program. This involves attempts to clarify the rationale, purpose, methods, concepts, and techniques of a program. These have been emphasized in connection with the appraisal approaches suggested here. Failure can be predicted for any organization that uses these systems of managerial appraisal, or any other approach, without placing means to achieve clarity at the highest priority.

Simplicity   Perhaps one of the best ways of assuring clarity is to avoid complexity. Certain soundly based management programs have lost their value to operating managers because they became too complex for people to understand. This has happened with the United States Defense Department administration of PERT and other systems approaches to planning and control. It can happen with managerial appraisal.

One of the ways of maintaining simplicity is to limit the use of forms and cut paper work to a minimum. Except for a few forms, suggested by the author and included in the Appendix, this book has dealt little with forms. Ideally, the best form is a blank sheet of paper and a checklist. However, in order to get objectives and manager appraisals in a way that they can be used, reviewed, and compared, some minimal forms, primarily giving guidelines, are necessary. If there is any caveat that should be given to those who would install a managerial appraisal program, it is to keep it as simple as possible, to make attempts to design simplicity into it and not complexity.

Integrating Appraisals with Management Selection and Development

Appraisal of managers is not an end unto itself. We do it for a purpose. The obvious reason is to assure that we have the most effective possible cadre of managers. The best kind of managerial appraisal will be tied into selection and development of managers. It ought also, as the section below will indicate, to be tied into compensation of managers.

Manager Selection One of the most difficult and risky tasks of a manager is the selection of incumbents for managerial posts. This is so at any level, but it becomes particularly difficult and risky the higher in the managerial hierarchy we go. It is difficult because we usually are not sure of the qualifications of available candidates. It is risky because a misfit in a managerial position cannot always be detected quickly — for top-level jobs it is seldom less than a year — with the result that losses in money are incurred through salary and inept managing, but the even larger loss in irreplaceable time is suffered.

To the extent that we can select incumbents for vacancies from within the company and to the extent that we do have a good appraisal system, we should select people on the basis of their appraised performance. This not only makes sense but it also will do much to give appraisal the status and significance it deserves.

Management Development While training of managers has emerged in the past two decades as one of the most widespread and costly forms of all education, there have been rumblings of disillusionment and dissatisfaction. Are we training for polish and elegance or results? Are we spending our time and money on the right people? What do people need to know and how much? Is the training related to the realities of operations for now and the future? Are we forgetting the utilization of perhaps the most effective training approach — the teaching of the subordinate by a knowledgeable superior — coaching?[4]

An effective managerial appraisal program should understandably give the key to management development. It should show who needs what kind of development. Indeed, it should be a development tool as well as an approach to appraisal.

[4] As Myles Mace said many years ago, "If we are to train a dog, however, we must know more than the dog."

Experience has shown that the two approaches outlined in this book do these things. They are easy to integrate with management development. They involve a way of doing things well. They give evidence on why people fail or succeed, why and where they miss, and where training is needed. Moreover, in the emphasis on accomplishment underlying both aspects of the appraisal program, they have built in a powerful source of motivating managers to undertake self-development.

Tying Appraisals to Compensation

One of the more contentious areas related to appraisals is whether they should be tied into compensation, particularly extras such as bonuses and stock options, although merit increases play a major part. It has been widely held by scholars of management and practicing managers that appraisal should be separated from considerations of compensation.

The argument is usually made that, if compensation is related to appraisals, the superior will tailor his appraisal to his recommendation for salary increases or other compensation. It is argued that he will first decide whether or not he wishes to (or feels he must, to keep peace in the family) recommend more compensation. Then he will make the appraisal high or low to support this recommendation.

That this has happened, there can be no doubt. Anyone with experience in management has seen it many times, and most of us have done it. But why? The main reason has been that appraisals have almost invariably been subjective in the past, and we can indeed tailor them to our recommendations. At best, salary and bonus decisions are one of the most difficult and distasteful parts of a superior manager's job, and the higher in the organization structure, the more difficult and unpleasant.

However, as evaluation systems become more objective and thorough, there is no reason why a direct tie should not exist between appraisal and compensation. The question may be put in this way: On what other basis than performance should compensation in any of its forms be awarded? There should be none, although unfortunately compensation is often given because someone has been loyal, has been with the company for a long time, everyone likes him, or he would be unhappy if an associate received a raise or a higher bonus than he did. Just recounting these lines of thinking and others that could be named shows how silly—albeit factual—they are.

Appraisal should lie at the base of a compensation program. But if it does, it must be as objective as possible. It is believed that the programs suggested in this book, along with the safeguards of review provided, are sufficiently objective and thorough to be used as the major basis of compensation.

An increasing, but still too few, number of companies that have been operating under a program of management by objectives have been basing compensation decisions, particularly with bonuses, on performance appraisal. For example, General Mills insists that bonus awards be made up or down from a "normal," depending upon an executive's verified performance against goals.

In actual operation, an advanced and effective bonus compensation plan was tied into the two-phase program presented in this book. In the company involved, a bonus plan was established providing for a bonus pool calculated each year as a given percentage of earnings before taxes after retention of a percentage for shareholders' equity and long-term borrowing (so that the top management could not gain bonus dollars by using borrowing rather than equity financing). This pool was first allocated on a provisional basis to each manager eligible for the plan by taking his annual salary, multiplying it by a factor from 1.0 to 1.5 to take into account the level of his responsibility, and then dividing the total adjusted salaries into the bonus pool. This first calculation resulted in a "presumed bonus" for each participant. It might vary in a given year from $1,000 for the lowest man in the program to $15,000 for the highest man. Then the results of appraisals of performance against verifiable objectives and performance as a manager were submitted up the line with superiors' reviews and recommendations for percentages over or above "presumed" bonus until they reached the Bonus Committee of the Board of Directors, consisting wholly of outside directors.

The Bonus Committee carefully reviewed the appraisals and recommendations, noted differences in rating discrimination, in recommendations, and in performance. On the basis of summarizing these factors and particularly outlining the strengths and weaknesses in each man's performance, the Bonus Committee then came to a determination of the actual bonus award which might be well above or below the presumed bonus. Its findings, along with the amount of the presumed bonus and the actual bonus and the reasons, were given to the person's immediate superior for discussion of the reasons for the bonus award. (For actual examples of such a summary, see Appendix 5.)

This kind of system has certain merits. In the first place, it puts evaluation in an important light that no other approach could—in affecting the dollars in a man's pocket. Secondly, by thorough review up the line, raters are put on notice that the quality of their evaluations must be defensible. Finally, by having an independent review committee make final reviews and awards, the problems of favoritism or the superior being a benevolent autocrat are greatly diminished.

But notice that compensation could not be safely tied to evaluation unless there were confidence that the evaluation was reasonably fair and thorough. Furthermore, the company did not intend, or risk the dangers of, secrecy in its bonus awards. Because there is seldom for long such a thing as a "confidential" payroll or bonus payment, companies who would make differences in salaries or bonuses or other forms of compensation based on performance should be prepared to give the specific reasons why. With an adequate and reasonably objective system of appraisal, this can be done. In the years of operation of this program and despite considerable discrimination in bonus awards, there has not been a single instance where it has come to light that any executive felt he had been unfairly treated. On the contrary, most executives, now fully aware of their deficiencies in meeting goals and performing as managers, have expressed surprise that they came out as well as they did.

In summary, then, it can be said that, contrary to popular opinion, compensation should be tied to evaluations. But to do this, evaluations must be acceptably objective and the program given a high order of attention.[5]

The Question of Tailoring Appraisals for Individual Enterprises

It is often said that any management technique or approach should be tailored to the situation to which it is applied. Certainly this is true with most control systems and techniques. It is likewise true that many management approaches should be tailored to the level of sophistication of the organization to which they are applied. Variable budgeting, for example,

---

[5] It is interesting that this position agrees with that of one of the world's foremost management compensation experts. In his book *Men, Money and Motivation* (New York: McGraw-Hill Book Company, 1961), on p. 216, Arch Patton supported this opinion, saying: "If performance appraisal is worthwhile, it should provide the backbone for executive personnel administration," and "for performance appraisal to be firmly rooted in a company's way of life it should play a key role in promotions, merit increases, and bonus payments."

can be based upon carefully researched and engineered standards to convert various volumes of operation into needs of every department for manpower, materials, and money. Or it can be based on crudely developed estimates of the variation or fixity of accounting costs, account by account. Capital budgeting can be attuned to rough calculations of savings, pay-back, or return on investment, or it can be made very exact and sophisticated by the use of advanced methods of discounted cash flow.

The same differences and the same degrees of tailoring are often believed to be applicable to managerial appraisal. However, looking at the program of evaluating performance against verifiable objectives along with that of appraising managers as managers, it is hard to see that much tailoring is necessary. Both deal with aspects of performance at so fundamental a level that they should be applicable to large and small businesses and to enterprises other than those in business.

To be sure, the quality and verifiability of objectives may differ. Success in recognizing and working out a network of goals may vary. But the approach of setting and appraising actual performance against objectives would not seem to require much tailoring. Likewise, in evaluating managers as managers, as was pointed out in the discussion of this program, certain key checklist points may vary in applicability or not be applicable at all in certain positions and enterprises. But, other than such modifications, this system would not appear to require extensive tailoring.

In other words, other than the improvement in use that should come with practice and sophistication, little or no tailoring should be required. This is due to the fact that all enterprises and every departmental segment should be designed to achieve objectives efficiently and effectively. Also, the fundamentals of managing are so universal that a system of appraising managers as managers should not vary in its basics between kinds of operations.

Managerial Appraisals and the Management Audit

One of the interesting possibilities in the development of management skill is the possibility of a management audit. This is an attempt to audit the quality of managing in a company or a major division as a total managerial system. The idea is that effective management is the best safeguard for the future for an investor, for a supplier who puts confidence in a company, or for a customer who wishes to assure himself of the long-run stability of an enterprise. It has even been suggested that the future may bring forward a certified management audit, an independent appraisal of a company's management by an outside firm.

Various pioneering approaches to this kind of audit have been made.[6] But this program, with all its advantages, has not made much progress, except for the occasional work of the Defense Department in evaluating the management of companies to which it contemplates giving an important defense contract and the infrequent work of a few management consulting firms.

One of the major reasons for lack of progress in developing management audits has been the fact that generally acceptable standards have been missing. Another reason has been the lack of independent firms equipped to undertake these audits, although a few of the major management consulting

[6] Noteworthy is the writing and work of Jackson Martindell in *The Scientific Appraisal of Management* (New York: Harper and Row, Publishers, Incorporated, 1950) and *The Appraisal of Management* (New York: Harper and Row, Publishers, Incorporated, 1962). Also see W. P. Leonard, *The Management Audit* (Englewood Cliffs, N.J.: Prentice-Hall, Inc., 1962), and W. T. Greenwood, *A Management Audit System* (Athens: Ohio University Press, 1964).

firms come close to offering this service. Perhaps another reason is that there has not been a pressing requirement for them, even though investors, at least, would probably be better protected with a good management audit than they are with an accounting audit.

As we approach the solution of managerial appraisal and develop techniques and standards that are believed to be accurate and workable, interest in management audits may be revived. There is much to be said for this possibility. Certainly boards of directors charged with the responsibility of seeing that a company is well managed should welcome it. And it should be only a short step from effective appraisal of individual managers to appraisal of an entire company's system of managing.

Filling the Requirements for an Effective Appraisal System

At the outset of this book, the requirements for an effective appraisal program were outlined. It will be recalled that these were: (1) the program should measure the right things; (2) the program should be operational; (3) the program should be objective; (4) the program should be acceptable; and (5) the program should be constructive. It is believed that the two-phase program suggested in this book meets these criteria fairly well.

Measuring the Right Things   The task of a manager is to manage his unit and company so that objectives are accomplished efficiently and effectively by those for whom he is responsible. Efficiently, in the sense that the minimum amount of time, material, money, and effort is expended. Effectively, in the sense that goals are actually achieved. Thus the task of managers is goal achievement. But since this must be done through the cooperative efforts of a group of people, their task also is to undertake managerial functions efficiently.

By setting up a program of evaluation that measures performance against preselected verifiable goals, objectives achievement is dealt with. By supplementing this program with an evaluation of performance as managers, the managerial role responsibilities are subjected to appraisal. Thus the suggested two-phase program, even with its imperfections and need for further refinement, is designed to measure the right things.

Making the Program Operational One of the criticisms long leveled at traditional appraisal schemes has been that they are not operational, in the sense that they are apart from what the manager actually does, separate from his day-to-day operations. Setting of objectives and means of reaching them are at the very core of any manager's job. Likewise, proficiency in managing will depend largely on how well he understands and applies the fundamentals of management. While there is more to managing than can be summarized in performance against objectives and the selected criteria of performance as a manager, it is believed that these two areas of measurement deal with enough critical areas of a manager's position to be adequate standards for measuring performance. In any case, the standards selected and the means of applying them for purposes of evaluation are certainly operational.

Making the Program Objective The essence of objectivity is the determination, with a minimum of uncertainty and judgment, of whether something has or has not been done. While there still exist elements of indefiniteness and subjectivity in the suggested approaches to managerial evaluation, it is certain that the two-phase system recommended here goes far in the right direction. Further research and experience can increase the degree of verifiability and objectivity, and it is believed this will happen.

Much of the problem of verifiability arises in the setting of qualitative goals. This takes practice and patient teaching. However, it can be done. Any objective of any clarity can be made highly verifiable and thereby responsive to highly objective measurement.

Making the Program Acceptable   One of the major advantages of appraising managers' performances against objectives is that these programs have become widely acceptable. People want to know what is expected of them, where they are going, and how they are doing. They like also the almost inevitable situation that occurs where they have a chance to contribute to setting objectives, an opportunity to clarify their authority, and the means of working out with their superior removal of obstructions to their performance. Every effective program of management by objectives, when done as suggested in this book, has shown great increases in morale and satisfaction.

Not enough experience has been had in the system of appraising managers as managers to be able to generalize on acceptance. Such experience as has been had does show a high degree of willingness to accept. People in managerial roles like to feel like managers and are almost universally interested in the nature and requirements of the task. To feel like a manager and to act like one requires some knowledge of what managing is and what the underlying principles and science of management involve. Some of this can be learned from attending seminars and reading books. But there is no learning experience better than living it, applying it to your own life and to the operations of those reporting to you.

Making the Program Constructive   Throughout this book the constructive nature of the suggested two-phase program has been repeatedly noted. Learning to set goals, clearing away the environment for their accomplishment and developing means of achieving them, and having a clear idea of what control information is needed to follow the stages of accomplishment are certainly constructive. Knowing that a person will be fairly and objectively appraised on the basis of these accomplishments not only gives an incentive for doing things well, but also gives a person the opportunity of knowing himself how well he is doing.

The learning and coaching aspects of appraising managers as managers have been emphasized. They furnish a means of helping people to become better managers. It is a rare person in a managerial position who does not want to become a better manager.

In general, then, appraisal as suggested here does, and should do, more than appraise. Effective appraisal alone is enough to justify a program, with the requirements for knowing what quality of manager a person is, and knowing whether he should be demoted or promoted, how he should be compensated, and what his development needs are. While this is enough, it is also desirable that an effective appraisal program help incumbents of managerial positions to do their jobs better and become better managers.

Selected Bibliography

Berkwitt, G. J.: "Formula for Measuring Executives," *Dun's Review,* vol. 92, no. 8, pp. 43–47 (August, 1968).

Coleman, C. J.: "Avoiding Pitfalls in Results Oriented Appraisals," *Personnel,* vol. 42, no. 6, pp. 24–33 (November–December, 1965).

Drucker, P. F.: *The Effective Executive* (New York: Harper and Row, Publishers, Incorporated, 1966).

———: *Managing for Results* (New York: Harper and Row, Publishers, Incorporated, 1964).

———: *The Practice of Management* (New York: Harper and Row, Publishers, Incorporated, 1954), chap. 11.

Drum, R. S.: "Performance Evaluation," *Personnel Journal,* vol. 38, no. 9, pp. 338–340 (February, 1960).

Enell, J. W., and G. H. Haas: *Setting Standards for Executive Performance* (New York: American Management Association, 1960).

Flanagan, J. C.: "The Critical Incident Technique," *Psychological Bulletin,* vol. 51, no. 4, pp. 327–358 (July, 1954).

Glasner, D. M.: "Patterns of Management by Results," *Business Horizons,* vol. 12, no. 1, pp. 37–40 (February, 1969).

Granger, C. H.: "How to Set Company Objectives," *Management Review,* vol. 59, no. 7, pp. 2–8 (July, 1970).

Heyel, C.: *Appraising Executive Performance* (New York: American Management Association, 1958).

Howell, R. A.: "A Fresh Look at Management by Objectives," *Business Horizons,* vol. 10, no.3, pp. 51–58 (Fall, 1967).

Hughes, C. L.: *Goal Setting* (New York: American Management Association, 1965).

———: "Why Goal Oriented Performance Reviews Succeed and Fail," *Personnel Journal,* vol. 45, no. 6, pp. 335–341 (June, 1966).

Humble, J. W.: *Improving Business Results* (London: McGraw-Hill Publishing Company, Ltd., 1968).

———(ed.): *Management by Objectives in Action* (London: McGraw-Hill Publishing Company, Ltd., 1970).

Kellogg, M. S.: "Appraising the Performance of Management Personnel: A Case Study," *Personnel,* vol. 31, no. 5, pp. 442–455 (March, 1955).

———: *What to Do about Performance Appraisal* (New York: American Management Association, 1965).

Kelly, P. R.: "Reappraisal of Appraisals," *Harvard Business Review,* vol. 36, no. 3, pp. 59–68 (May–June, 1958).

Kindell, A. F., and J. Gatza: "Positive Program for Performance Appraisal," *Harvard Business Review,* vol. 41, no. 6, pp. 153–160 (November–December, 1963).

Labovitz, G. H.: "In Defense of Subjective Executive Appraisal," *Academy of Management Journal,* vol. 12, no. 3, pp. 293–307 (September, 1969).

Levinson, H.: "Management by Whose Objectives?" *Harvard Business Review,* vol. 48, no. 4, pp. 125–134 (July–August, 1970).

Mahler, W. R., and G. Frazier: "Appraisal of Executive Performance: The Achilles Heel of Management Development," *Personnel,* vol. 31, no. 5, pp. 429–441 (March, 1955).

Mayfield, H.: "In Defense of Performance Appraisal," *Harvard Business Review,* vol. 38, no. 2, pp. 81–87 (March–April, 1960).

McConkey, D. D.: *How to Manage by Results* (New York: American Management Association, 1965).

McGregor, D.: "An Uneasy Look at Performance Appraisal," *Harvard Business Review,* vol. 35, no. 3, pp. 89–94 (May–June, 1957).

Meyer, H. H., E. Kay, and J. R. P. French, Jr.: "Split Roles in Performance Appraisal," *Harvard Business Review,* vol. 43, no. 1, pp. 123–129 (January–February, 1965).

Miller, E. C.: *Objectives and Standards: An Approach to Planning and Control* (New York: American Management Association, 1966).

———: *Objectives and Standards of Performance in Financial Management* (New York: American Management Association, 1968).

———: *Objectives and Standards of Performance in Marketing Management* (New York: American Management Association, 1967).

———: *Objectives and Standards of Performance in Production Management* (New York: American Management Association, 1967).

Miner, J. B.: "Management Appraisal: A Capsule Review and Current References," *Business Horizons,* vol. 11, no. 5, pp. 83–93 (October, 1968).

Odiorne, G. S.: *Management by Objectives* (New York: Pitman Publishing Corporation, 1965).

Patton, A.: "How To Appraise Executive Performance," *Harvard Business Review,* vol. 38, no. 1, pp. 63–70 (January–February, 1960).

Payne, B. L.: "An Appraisal of Managers and Management Development," *Management Record,* vol. 23, no. 3, pp. 8–17 (March, 1961).

Raia, A. P.: "Goal Setting and Self-control," *Journal of Management Studies,* vol. 2, no. 1, pp. 34–53 (February, 1965).

———: "A Second Look at Management Goals and Controls," *California Management Review,* vol. 8, no. 4, pp. 49–58 (Summer, 1966).

Randle, C. W., and W. H. Monroe: "Better Ways to Measure Executive Performance," *Management Methods,* January, 1961, pp. 64ff.

Rowland, V. K.: *Evaluating and Improving Managerial Performance* (New York: McGraw-Hill Book Company, 1970).

Schleh, E. C.: *Management by Results* (New York: McGraw-Hill Book Company, 1961).

Tosi, H. L., and S. J. Carroll: "Managerial Reaction to Management by Objectives," *Academy of Management Journal,* vol. 1, no. 4, pp. 415–426 (December, 1968).

Tosi, H. L., J. R. Rizzo, and S. J. Carroll: "Setting Goals in Management by Objectives," *California Management Review,* vol. 12, no. 4, pp. 70–78 (Summer, 1970).

Valentine, R. F.: *Performance Objectives for Managers* (New York: American Management Association, 1966).

Whisler, T. L., and S. F. Harper (eds.): *Performance Appraisal: Research and Practice* (New York: Holt, Rinehart and Winston, Inc., 1962).

Wikstrom, W. S.: *Developing Managerial Competence: Changing Concepts, Emerging Practices* (New York: National Industrial Conference Board, Inc., 1964).

———: *Managing by—and with—Objectives* (New York: National Industrial Conference Board, Inc., 1968).

———: "Setting Targets for Staff," *Conference Board Record,* vol. 1, no. 10, pp. 32–34 (October, 1964).

Williams, A. P. O.: "Increasing the Value of Management Appraisal Schemes: An Organizational Learning Approach," *Journal of Management Studies,* vol. 7, no. 1, pp. 23–36 (February, 1970).

Examples of Appraisal
of Performance
against Objectives

*(Excerpts from Various Positions
with Evaluation Comments)*

Appendix I-A

PERFORMANCE AGAINST VERIFIABLE OBJECTIVES

Division General Manager Report on Sales and Costs
in Small Division

PERFORMANCE AGAINST GOALS

Date: February 13, 1970

PARTICIPANT: M. E. Jones, General Manager   DIVISION: Special Tools   Report for: Year End

SALES & PROFITS By: Product Line:	GOALS				ACCOMPLISHMENT 1969		
	Sales	Units	Gross Profit	GP %	Sales	Gross Profit	GP %
	(000's)		(000's)		(000's)	(000's)	
Private Label A	$ 500		$ 184	37.1	$ 985	$ 288	29.2
Private Label B	152		56	37.1	192	64	33.3
Private Label C	124		44	37.1	25	8	32.0
Private Label D	852		316	37.1	785	223	28.4
Private Label – Other	480		176	37.1	587	141	24.0
Product A	800		296	37.1	805	315	39.1
Product B	300		112	37.1	318	130	40.9
Product C	1,001		373	37.1	957	276	28.8
Product D	200		76	37.1	171	56	32.7
Product E	–		–	–	2	1	50.0
Product F	237		90	37.1	3	1	33.3
Total New Products*	237		90	37.1	3	1	33.3
Miscellaneous							
TOTAL:	$4,646		$1,723	37.1	$4,830(+4%)	$1,503(−12.7%)	31.1

*All new products were Product F above.

| | | GOALS | | ACCOMPLISHMENT | | | |
| | | | | ACTUAL | | (OVER) UNDER | |
BURDEN & PERIOD EXPENSES		Amount (000's)	Percent to Sales	Amount (000's)	Percent to Sales	Amount (000's)	Percent
Burden	Plant 1	$ 121	2.6	$ 151	3.1	$(30)	(25)
	Plant 2	87	1.9	83	1.7	(4)	(5)
Mfg.—	Plant 1	62	1.3	61	1.3	1	2
General Admin.	Plant 2	25	.5	22	.5	3	14
Materiel	Plant 1	69	1.5	72	1.5	(3)	(4)
	Plant 2	24	.5	41	.8	(17)	(71)
Marketing	Plant 1	220	4.7	183	3.8	37	20
	Plant 2	81	1.7	88	1.8	(7)	(9)
Engineering	Plant 1	54	1.2	78	1.6	(24)	(44)
	Plant 2	24	.5	35	.7	(11)	(46)
G & A*	Plant 1	110	2.4	130	2.6	(20)	(18)
	Plant 2	18	.4	28	.6	(10)	(56)
R&D		83	1.8	73	1.5	10	14
Bldgs. & Grds.		202	4.4	226	4.7	(24)	(11)
TOTAL		$1,180	25.4	$1,271	26.3	$(91)	(8)
Divisional Operating Product		534	11.7	232	4.8	311	59

*Divisional G & A included in plant 1.

Participant: M. E. Jones   Date: 2-13-70

PERFORMANCE AGAINST GOALS IN 1969

SALES BY PRODUCT LINE

Private Label A

This account nearly met the million-dollar net sales figure. Fourth quarter remains strong with $266,000 in sales. During the last six months of the year, we definitely were rewarded for our price reduction in March. We picked up an extra $100,000 of business in the second half of the year, which is exactly one-half of what the customer predicted our increase would be when they added Detroit, Cleveland, and St. Louis to our coverage. The gross profit percentage of 29.2 per cent, while below our average break-even gross, is not completely without value for the amount of volume involved. Goal exceeded in net sales and gross profit dollars.

Private Label B

Quarterly sales increased slightly to $51,000. This account has been rather steady in their quarterly purchases throughout the entire year. One additional product still has not entered their line. They are having internal problems and shake-ups in their marketing department. This product line exceeded net sales and gross profit dollar goals.

Private Label C

This account has discontinued purchasing from us, except on very rare occasions. We were not in a position to aggressively counterattack, but we anticipate that we will make some inroads in this area during fiscal 1970. This category did not meet net sales or gross profit goals.

Private Label D

Sales for fourth quarter continued to average slightly above $70,000 monthly, much as third quarter of 1969. This is a considerable improvement over the first six months of the year. This was also true despite the fact that there was some slowing down in their activities toward the latter part of the year in anticipation of taking on a new line of products beginning in 1970. Missed sales goal by $67,000 after a very shaky start. Believe we have recaptured customer confidence and we're convinced they have the sales team to do the job. Anticipate a banner year in this area in 1970.

Private Label—Other

This category had a strong fourth quarter. The average per quarter for the first nine months was $139,000, and we hit $170,000 for the fourth quarter. The bulk of the gain came from business with new customer X. We obtained $100,000 worth of business from them in the fourth quarter. This, coupled with $183,000 for the first nine months, put them over the quarter-million-dollar mark for the entire year. Despite this strong performance, we are somewhat apprehensive about 1970 since we believe that their new product approach will eat into the conventional market and sales will probably diminish as a result. We have tried to interest them in our similar new product, but they are satisfied with the material they started with. Now we're hoping to get them involved in our new system to offset our losses that we feel will be forthcoming.

Customer Y had a strong year with us, doing $133,000, and we anticipate that we will top that mark considerably for 1970.

The only company showing any appreciable decline for fourth quarter was customer Z, but their dollar volume is not as substantial so we were not hurt very badly as a result.

Profit margin in this area is the lowest of any of our marketing categories. We definitely intend to increase prices and are hopeful that we can slide them up, although we are concerned that it could upset our business picture. Private label sales for 1969 greatly exceeded forecast. Gross profit, however, was $35,000 under projection. I feel that the projections were wholly unrealistic in the gross profit area.

Product A

Disappointing during fourth quarter, dropping to quarterly average of $188,000 versus $208,000 average first three quarters. Field men continued to report that we are on the high end of the price scale. There are scattered reports from the Eastern Division that the product is not performing as consistently as desired in special work. We have an investigation taking place on this matter because we want to eliminate any possibility that this can contribute to any decline in sales in this area. Probably our largest single difficulty is the lack of field coverage in the southeastern portion of the United States. We expect that it will be rectified shortly and that our sales picture will straighten up accordingly. We did exceed our projections in net sales and profitability in this line for 1969. Gross profit rose 0.9 per cent from the third quarter. This was due to over-accruals in anticipation of customers taking cash discounts. This accrual was reversed in the fourth quarter, which improved our gross margins.

Product B

We regret to report that the division has not done nearly as well with these accounts as our sister division did when they were handling them. They were averaging nearly $86,000 a quarter when they had them. We were able to do $60,000 in the fourth quarter. It is likely that we have not made contact with every single one of the accounts turned over to us, and we expect to apply intensive pressure to improve our situation. Furthermore, we lost perhaps the largest single account they were covering, due to a changeover on the part of the customer from the product he was previously using to a new system and our product did not satisfy him to the extent that our major competitor's did. This account alone did $41,000 worth of business with us in the first nine months, but only $150 for the last quarter. The category as a whole, however, exceeded net sales and gross profit dollar projections.

Product C

This category experienced a modest decline from the yearly average in the fourth quarter. Although we have instituted price increases on approximately fifteen materials sold in this area, the effect of them apparently has not been felt since our gross margin did not improve during the fourth quarter as a result of the increases. We anticipate additional price increases and thinning of the product line for 1970. Net sales and gross profit dollars were below projections for 1969.

Product D

While quarterly sales dropped to $42,000 which was less than the $50,000 for the third quarter, it is still above the quarterly average for the first six months and amounts to just about the quarterly average for the entire year. Despite the introduction of new products which are continuing to sell with improved margin situations, our overall margin in this area declined. This was due to the nature of the product mix for the period. Net sales and gross profit dollars both were below projections for this category for the year.

Product E

We are out of this business and will not be reporting on it in 1970.

Product F

We finally made our breakthrough. We had our first small sales, of $3,000, during the month of September and considerably more is anticipated during the year 1970. The equipment is in, we have experienced problems with the presses not being able to handle the production rate, and we will require some changes in that regard, but overall, we are highly optimistic and enthusiastic about the future for this area of business. We were well below net sales and gross profit projections for this category for 1969.

Total New Products

Remarks regarding Product F activity applicable here as above, and they account for much of our miss on new products.

Total

Net sales for the year ended up $184,000 ahead of our projections. Because of operational costs and unattractive margins in various product lines, we were unable to achieve the overall gross profit percentage we were seeking. As a result, we were $220,000 under our gross profit dollar estimate. Our sales gain was higher in the fourth quarter than the average for the balance of the year, and our gross profit dollar deficiency was slightly less than the deficiency experienced for the first nine months of the year. Our net sales gain is approximately 11.2 percent over calendar year 1968. The year 1968 produced divisional operating income of $6,000. Preliminary figures from accounting indicate 1969 was $232,000 with possibly as much as another $50,000–$60,000 falling into this area as a result of unused inventory reserve being credited back to income. Divisional operating income was $27,000 for the year when present management assumed responsibility for the division. During the remaining two-thirds of the year, that income rose an additional $205,000. The latter figure would be even higher if we had not elected to write off a substantial amount of materials which had accumulated on the premises over the last four years. These were products no longer useable.

COMMENTS ON OPERATING EXPENSES

Burden

The burden account for the fourth quarter showed a substantial increase in both plants. These increases were greater than increases in volume. They were due primarily to the following:

In plant 1, we had two motor repairs of slightly over $1,600. We paid employees for sick time which they had not taken off. This was $1,450. The pay increase that applied to burden accounts represented approximately another $1,350. We had changes in our Quality Control Department which amounted to salary increases of $600 for the quarter, and we continued to have very heavy demands on our Maintenance Department. A lot of this was due to installation of manufacturing equipment and the new presses which arrived in the December period. Our Maintenance overruns, alone, for the fourth quarter were about $8,500. The items enumerated account for most of our overrun for the year. The balance was scattered among small miscellaneous supply and maintenance part items.

Our plant 2 facility also suffered an increase in their burden factor. They had been performing very well up to this point in time. They went over by $9,000 for the fourth quarter. They were affected by a breakdown in the mill. This breakdown cost us over $2,000 to get the mill repaired, and there was additional time involved since we worked a third shift and staggered our activities with people having to cover for each other to the extent that we had to pay a fair amount of premium time.

Burden expenses should continue to run high through the first quarter of

1970, as there are still a fair amount of pieces of equipment coming into both facilities which will draw heavily on our maintenance ability.

Manufacturing–General Administrative
Performance in this area was satisfactory with plant 1 holding its position from past report and plant 2 improving its situation by $3,000.

Materiel
Plant 1 was able to improve its performance during the fourth quarter, and we held the line without any further slippage. Plant 2's performance in this area dropped $17,000 from the goals established. Most of this was due to office supplies, small tools and equipment, and rental of equipment, all of which were items for which there was no amount provided in the 1969 operational budget.

Marketing
There was an additional gain in this account of $17,000 in the plant 1 area during the fourth quarter, this despite the fact that we have added to our Marketing Department. We have been watching our other expenditures very carefully, especially items relating to advertising and sales promotion.
Plant 2, which had been doing a very poor job of staying within budget, improved its budget position by $1,000 during the fourth quarter. Expenses in this area can be expected to increase in 1970 since we have a definite need to improve our marketing strength. I think our sales accomplishments for the entire year, based on the amount of money allocated, were considerable, and I believe the people in the field are to be commended for their efforts.

Engineering
This department has had a continued increase in overexpenditure. Again, this is due to the fact that our consultant has been charged to this department but was not budgeted in the department, and during the month of December he received an additional $2,500 lump-sum payment. The plant 2 overage is due to the addition of one man and the correct charging of another into this category rather than Quality Control.

G & A
Both plant areas were over budget $2,000 for the fourth quarter, which was an improvement in performance over any of the prior three quarters during the year. Department F470, Division General Management, shows an overspent position of $19,683 for the year. Of this, $27,040 is an account used by the Accounting Department to charge off discrepancies resulting from my predecessor's adjusting budgets after settling on a profit plan. The combined telephone and TWX service budget was off about $3,000 for the year, and there was an overage of about $3,700 in employment agency fees which were inadequately provided for. The

balance of accounts looks very sound, and there were some large offsetting pluses which we did not use that tended to throw the picture on the whole onto the plus side. Plant 1's overage of $11,000 is primarily due to a $2,700 overcharge in office supplies, $2,800 for office equipment rentals for which nothing was provided in the budget, some personnel preemployment fees for which there was no budgetary provision, and some fringe benefit recharges of $603, plus outside clerical help of $1,270. As pointed out earlier, the retrogression in this area is less than that occurring during the early part of the year.

R&D

This department's position continued to improve during the balance of the year even though we added a key man to the staff. However, we did not charge him immediately into this particular account number, and he is taking on a function which is kind of a combination of development and technical supervision.

Buildings and Grounds

This has slipped another $11,000 during the last quarter. Our general liability insurance in plant 1 ended up at $25,517 for the year, and $27,102 in plant 2. Neither of these was provided for in the budget. As a matter of fact, it would appear that there was no budgetary provision for insurance such as boiler machinery, auto and travel and accident. Personal property taxes appear to be more than adequately taken care of in the plant 1 area where we have a $48,000 plus factor which accounts for any balance or offset that we enjoy in this account number. The plant 2 area, on the other hand, was $3,727 over in personal property taxes. A substantial adjusting entry of $51,796 for plant 2 during the month of December was the basis for bringing that area's buildings and grounds account into balance. Utility estimates were fairly accurate. Plant 1 ran $68 under budget for the year. Plant 2 was $1,805 over. Some of that was probably due to the necessity of operating the third shift as a result of our mill breakdown.

Total

We ended the year $91,000 over our goal in burden and period expenses. The burden, general and administrative, and engineering departments were the worst contributors to the problem. In addition, in the plant 1 area there was a decline in the average production during the last quarter versus the first nine months of the year, but the overall work force remained relatively stable. Of course, December was a very difficult month to obtain production because of our limited number of working days due to holidays and inventory taking. In addition, there was a great deal of emphasis in both facilities on elimination of the spoiled materials, and a fair amount of manpower had to be devoted to culling these out and taking the necessary steps to dispose of them. It is not anticipated that this distortion will carry through the 1970 year. Although the $232,000 divisional profit is considerably less than we had anticipated, it is much better than calendar year 1968. Preliminary information from the accounting department indicates there may be $65,000–$75,000 that can be added to this figure as a result of reversing reserves which were not needed. For example, in 1968 we suffered a $105,000 discrepancy between our book inventory and the physical. Preliminary indication this year shows that the figure may be closer to $4,000. Reserves were provided for $60,000 as a result of last year's experience. If we find the $4,000 holds up, this alone would add $56,000 to the divisional net income. We do believe that the overall result will show that the division has improved its profitability picture from $250,000 to $280,000 over that of calendar year 1968. We are anticipating that further programs which are already in the works will give us additional improvement in this area in 1970, and despite the depressed economic forecast, we anticipate a better year.

QUANTITATIVE AND QUALITATIVE GOALS
FOR MIDDLE-MANAGEMENT POSITIONS

Participant: <u>S. E. Clark, Operations Manager</u>   Division: <u>Chemical</u>

Quantitative
VERIFIABLE GOAL NO.: <u>   1   </u>   Target Date for
Accomplishment

Brief Statement:	$12,500 by end of 1st quarter.
Objective to save $50,000 at plant 1 and plant 2 combined by instituting savings measures, such as purchasing used drums instead of new, contracting solvent purchases for both plants at lower prices, plus other purchasing reforms to reduce raw material costs substantially.	$25,000 by end of 2nd quarter. $37,500 by end of 3rd quarter. $50,000 by end of 1969.
Results Expected:	
A minimum saving of $50,000	

1st Quarter Review:

Successful in capturing $12,555 in savings.

Some details:	(a) Savings in drum purchases	$ 7,077
	(b) Savings in solvent purchases	580
	(c) Savings in miscellaneous raw materials	3,527
	(d) Savings in lids and cans	1,371
	Total savings	$12,555

2nd Quarter Review:

Successful in capturing $18,372 in savings.

Summary of savings:	(a) Savings in purchases of drums	$ 9,900
	(b) Savings in purchases of solvents	897
	(c) Savings in miscellaneous raw materials	5,757
	(d) Savings in purchases of packaging supplies	1,838
	Total savings	$18,392

3rd Quarter Review:

Successful in capturing $19,883 in savings versus objective of $12,500.

Summary of savings:	(a) Savings in purchases of drums	$9,385
	(b) Savings in purchases of solvents	5,160

(c)	Savings on latex purchases	2,080
(d)	Savings on purchases of misc. raw materials	1,758
(e)	Savings on cans and cartons	1,500
	Total savings	$19,883
	Total savings for first 3 qrtrs.	$50,810

4th Quarter Review:

Successful in capturing $17,371 in savings versus objective of $12,500.

Summary of savings:	(a) Savings in purchases of drums	$ 7,813
	(b) Savings in purchases of solvents	5,575
	(c) Savings on latex purchases	1,912
	(d) Savings on purchases misc. raw materials	1,847
	(e) Savings on cans and cartons	224
	Total savings	$17,371
	Total savings for 1969	$68,201

Superior's Comments:

We experienced a decline in savings and purchases of drums for the fourth quarter because of an increase in prices of new drums. However, the savings over 1968 are still appreciable. Our solvent contract is continuing to pay off. Our latex savings should go up as soon as we complete the installation of our transfer equipment. We have also experienced price increases in certain container and carton sizes which have almost equalized any prior savings. Despite the general escalation in costs, I think Clark did an outstanding job in meeting this objective. He exceeded the goal by $18,201 for the year.

GOALS AND OBJECTIVES

Participant: S. E. Clark, Operations Manager   Division: Chemical

VERIFIABLE GOAL NO.: _____4_____ | Target Date for Accomplishment

Brief Statement:	
Determine for Product Manager by more accurate cost studies those products that he should evaluate for mar-	End of 2nd quarter.

keting program. This is to be done through completing
revision of standard cost and determination of gross
profits by product and by container size.

1st Quarter Review:

Initial cost studies at plant 1 and plant 2 complete. We are using outside
data processing firm to program and give results. Input data for program
completed in "first stage." Results expected for presentation to Marketing
Director (Product Manager) in 2nd quarter.

2nd Quarter Review:

Failure to accomplish data processing runs, either in outside firm or our
own corporate facility, has delayed cost study program on individual products. However, program now energized and results expected for presentation
to marketing group in 3rd quarter.

3rd Quarter Review:

We are now back to reprogramming. Former cost data now nearly one year
old. We are gathering new input cost data on raw materials and packaging
supplies. Corporate Cost Accounting has target date for standard costs of
December, 1969.

4th Quarter Review:

Have completed the standard costs of twenty-eight adhesive products on
December 9, 1969. However, there is considerable corrective work yet to be
accomplished by our Cost Accounting and Data Processing Divisions before
figures can be used with reliability. Believe I must share responsibility with
other corporate management that, collectively, we have not progressed on
the objective as well as is desirable.

Superior's Comments:

This objective not complete in useable form. This division has done a great
deal of work to bring us into a meaningful system, considering that we still
must rely on estimated labor costs. Unfortunately, the Financial Department
has not had the manpower to be as responsive as required. As a result, we
cannot accomplish our program on schedule.

Participant: Frank E. Burke, Sales Manager	Division: Building Products
VERIFIABLE GOAL NO.: 1	Target Date for Accomplishment
Brief Statement: *Establish Do-It-Yourself Market* A. Develop package designed to market through co-	April 1

operating hardware manufacturers, to make available to their distributors under a private label.	
B. Develop complete program, including merchandising rack, to promote do-it-yourself products.	July 1
C. Sales on this program will total $300,000 with a gross profit of $105,000.	December 31

Results Expected:

1st Quarter Review:

The package has been developed. It will be made available to cooperating manufacturers in June and to our distributors in August. We now expect sales of $225,000 with a gross margin of 45%, giving us a gross profit of $68,250.

Superior's Comments:

2nd Quarter Review:

The package, in a rough stage, was shown to three manufacturers in June. They expressed great interest and the Assistant Sales Manager will have a complete package with him on trip to manufacturers latter part of August or early part of September. The complete package with merchandise rack will be introduced to the District Sales Managers at the sales meeting in October and immediately following to the distributors. Sales are now expected to reach $180,000 with a gross profit of $51,000.

Superior's Comments: Essentially dates have been met (parts A and B). Sales (part C) must await December 31 for evaluation.—LEJ

3rd Quarter Review:

The complete package was introduced to the DSM's at the sales meeting. It appears that because of deliveries on the part of the vendors, we will not be in a position to introduce this product to distributors until the middle of December. After considering the value of a mid-December introduction, I am going to hold this product line until the January Markets to get the full impact. The result is that we will have no sales in this year and I will not have reached my objective.

Superior's Comments: Agree—goal not accomplished.—LEJ

4th Quarter Review:

As outlined in the 3rd Quarter Review, we withheld the introduction of this product line until the January Market. As a result, there were no sales for 1969. Initial results from market introduction indicate we will exceed our forecasts and could total as much as $800,000 for 1970.

Superior's Comments: This project, although behind Frank's schedule,

was launched in excellent fashion and promises
results well in excess of his forecast in 1970.—LEJ

Participant: Frank Burke, Sales Manager	Division: Building Products
VERIFIABLE GOAL NO.: 2	Target Date for Accomplishment

Brief Statement: *Hard Surface Tools and Adhesives*	
A. Develop specific tools and adhesives which will make company a single source for all types of installation materials.	April 1
1. Determine need for specific tools and adhesives. Resolve what tools to be manufactured by company and which are to be buy-out items, also locating source. Provide Chemical Division with information to develop adhesive.	
B. Introduce hard surface tools and adhesive to distributors.	July 1
C. With 100 distributors participating, sales will exceed $150,000 on tools and $150,000 on adhesives, with a gross profit of $70,000 on both.	

1st Quarter Review:

I am unable to introduce this line this year as planned. Earliest introduction will be at the 1970 January Market. On the tools, we can expect a gross of 20% and on the adhesives 25%. No sales are forecast for this fiscal year, but we expect sales of $300,000 for first year of introduction.

2nd Quarter Review:

Prices on all hard surface tools have been received as buy-out from Smith Company, giving us a gross profit of 20%. We are still planning an introduction at 1970 January Market, and no sales are forecast this year.

Superior's Comments: Goal not achieved and apparently will not be during fiscal 1969.—LEJ

3rd Quarter Review:

Although most of the information has been gathered on this line of products, it appears that the earliest target date for the introduction would be the January Markets, and no sales are forecast for this year.

Superior's Comments: Goal not achieved and apparently will not be during fiscal 1969.—LEJ

4th Quarter Review:

After a final study of this product line, it was decided not to add the tools to our line because the business is so fragmented. Chemical is now working on formulas to provide us with a complete line by June.

Superior's Comments: Not accomplished.—LEJ

Introduction and Form
for Appraisal
of Performance
as a Manager

Introduction and Form for Appraisal of Performance as a Manager

While appraisal of performance against goals is a tremendous step forward in manager appraisal, it is still subject to some of the problems of luck. In other words, it is entirely possible that a manager might reach or fail to reach goals largely due to circumstances beyond his control. Likewise, it is possible that proper goals might be difficult to establish. Also, setting verifiable goals, particularly for purposes of managerial appraisal, may overemphasize short-term goals at the expense of the long-term. Therefore, it would appear to be useful to have an individual assessed upon his ability to manage effectively.

By utilizing the basic principles of management and translating them into questions which can be used as guides and which can be answered with a fairly high degree of objectivity, insight can be gained in assessing *managerial* abilities.

In utilizing the following manager appraisal program it must be borne in mind that it is an experimental program. However, experience with it over five years in the middle and upper levels of a multinational company has indicated that (1) it is an aid to operating managers in understanding the basic nature of managing and (2) it does lend an acceptable degree of objectivity to assessing managerial competence.

Basic Considerations   To assist in using this tool, several things should be emphasized:

1. It is designed to apply only to persons who are in a managerial position; while some of the items are useful in applying to individuals without managerial responsibility (managerial responsibility applies to individuals who have subordinates and are, therefore, responsible for their work), many are not.

2. Raters are expected to mark with an *X* items which are *not* applicable to a given position.

3. A rater is not expected to know the answers to all questions on every individual reporting to him, but it is hoped that he will look for information on this item where he may not know. Where he does not know, he should mark the item with an *N*.

4. While the ideal rating system is one where questions are completely objective, it is recognized that people will vary in their competence on individual items; therefore, there is an element of subjectivity in rating individual questions. In this connection, it can be said that a manager's superior will be influenced by discrimination shown in rating by the rater.

5. It is recognized that certain questions apply to managerial fundamentals that are more important than others; but to reduce the complexity and subjectivity of this rating program, individual questions are not weighted. However, those in charge of final reviews will take into account ratings on the more important questions and areas.

6. Since the process of managing is a closely interlocked system, a rater may start with any part of this program. If he prefers, there is no harm done in starting with Control and working backwards to Planning.

Rating System In rating each question, give the following marks for each (for each level of rating use only one of two numbers, such as 4.0 or 4.5 for *Excellent,* not other decimals).

X = Not applicable to position.

N = Do not know accurately enough for rating.

5.0 = *Superior:* a standard of performance which could not be improved upon under any circumstances or conditions known to the rater.

4.0 or 4.5 = *Excellent:* a standard of performance which leaves little of any consequence to be desired.

3.0 or 3.5 =   *Good:* a standard of performance above the average and meeting all normal requirements of the position.

2.0 or 2.5 =   *Average:* a standard of performance regarded as average for the position involved and the people available.

1.0 or 1.5 =   *Fair:* a standard of performance which is below the normal requirements of the position, but one that may be regarded as marginally or temporarily acceptable.

0.0   =   *Inadequate:* a standard of performance regarded as unacceptable for the position involved.

In averaging ratings for any area, *average only the questions rated,* excluding the not applicable questions (*X*) and those on which you have inadequate information to rate *(N).*

PERFORMANCE AS A MANAGER

(Numbers in parentheses refer to appropriate pages in the fourth edition of Koontz and O'Donnell, *Principles of Management:* McGraw-Hill Book Company, 1968.)

PLANNING	RATING

1. Does he set for his departmental unit both short-term and long-term goals in verifiable terms (either qualitative or quantitative) that are related in a positive way to those of his superior and his company? (Pp. 84–85, 94, 111–121, 484–486, 488–501.) _____

2. To what extent does he make sure that the goals of his department are understood by those who report to him? (Pp. 120–121.) _____

3. How well does he assist those who report to him in establishing verifiable and consistent goals for their operations? (Pp. 120–121.) _____

4. To what extent does he utilize consistent and approved planning premises in his planning and see that his subordinates do likewise? (Pp. 94–96, 123–151.) _____

5. Does he understand the role of company policies in his decision making and assure that his subordinates do likewise? (Pp. 85–89, 177–197.) _____

6. Does he attempt to solve problems of subordinates by policy guidance, coaching, and encouragement of innovation, rather than by rules and procedures? (Pp. 85–89, 215.) _____

7. Does he help his subordinates get the information they need to assist them in their planning? (Pp. 200–201.) _____

8. To what extent does he seek out applicable alternatives before making a decision? (Pp. 152–153.) _____

9. In choosing from among alternatives, does he recognize and give primary attention to those factors which are limiting, or critical, to the solution of a problem? (Pp. 153–155.) _____

10. In making decisions, how well does he bear in mind the size and length of commitment involved in each decision? (Pp. 99–104.) _____

11. Does he check his plans periodically to see if they are still consistent with current expectations? (Pp. 105–106.) _____

12. To what extent does he consider the need for, as well as the cost of, flexibility in arriving at a planning decision? (Pp. 104–106, 224.) _____

13. In developing and implementing his plans, does he regularly consider longer-range implications of his decisions along with the shorter-range results expected? (Pp. 99–221.) _____

14. When he submits problems to his superior, or when a superior seeks help from him in solving problems, does he submit considered analyses of alternatives (with advantages and disadvantages) and recommend suggestions for solution? (Pp. 293–294, 324.) _____

Total number of questions on which ratings are made: _____
Total score on questions given ratings: _____
Average of ratings in PLANNING: _____

ORGANIZING   RATING

1. Does the organization structure under his control reflect major result areas? (Pp. 232–239.) _____

2. Does he delegate authority to his subordinates in accordance with results expected of them? (P. 75.) _____

3. Does he make his delegations clear (rather than detailed)? (Pp. 68–69, 407–408, 417–421.) _____

4. Does he formalize in writing his subordinates' position guides, authority delegations, and goals? _____

5. Does he clarify responsibilities for contributions to his programs? _____

6. Does he maintain adequate control when delegating authority? (Pp. 66, 374–375.) _____

7. Does he exact commensurate responsibility when he delegates authority? (P. 409.) _____

8. When he has delegated authority to his subordinate, does he refrain from making decisions in that area? (Pp. 71, 74.) _____

9. Does he take steps to make sure that his own subor-

dinates are properly delegating their authority where
necessary? (Pp. 368–375.)

10. Does he maintain unity of command or disregard it only
when the advantages of doing so clearly offset the disadvantages? (Pp. 74–75.)

11. Does he utilize staff advice when necessary and then
only as advice? (Pp. 296–297.)

12. Does he regularly teach to his subordinates, or otherwise make sure his subordinates understand, the nature
of line and staff relationships? (Pp. 291–301, 321–325.)

13. Does he limit and make crystal clear functional authority delegations in writing in his departments? (Pp. 301–
309, 317, 409–410.)

14. Does he use service departments only when it is clear
that control is required or efficiency will be enhanced
beyond the costs and dangers of inadequate service?
(Pp. 343–345.)

15. Does he take care not to create excessive levels of organization? (Pp. 243–245, 252–254.)

16. Does he exercise care not to use committees or group
meetings to make decisions that could be better made by
individuals? (Pp. 389–391, 397–399.)

17. Does he make sure that committee or group meetings
are preceded by proper agenda, information gathering,
analyses, and concrete proposals? (Pp. 400–404.)

18. Does he distinguish in his operations between lines of
authority and lines of information? (P. 408.)

19. Does he plan his organization structure so that he can
select and develop individuals who can meet future
organization requirements? (Pp. 412–417.)

Total number of questions on which ratings are made:
Total score of questions given ratings:
Average of ratings in ORGANIZING:

STAFFING   RATING

1. Does he take full responsibility for the staffing of his
department, even though he obtains needed assistance
from the personnel department? (Pp. 442–445.)

2. Does he make it clear to his subordinates that every position in his department is open to the best qualified individual, either inside or outside the company? (Pp. 448–451.)   ———

3. Does he take steps to make certain that his subordinates are given opportunity for training for better positions, both in his operations and elsewhere in the company? (Pp. 442–453, 508–515.)   ———

4. Does he utilize appropriate methods of training and developing his subordinates? (Pp. 507–515.)   ———

5. Does he effectively practice coaching of subordinates as a means of training? (Pp. 524–526.)   ———

6. Does he tend to keep subordinates who have questionable ability in their jobs?   ———

7. How well is he echeloned in his position?   ———

8. Does he appraise his subordinates objectively and regularly on the basis of performance against preselected goals? (Pp. 484–501.)   ———

9. Does he appraise his subordinates objectively and regularly on their ability to manage effectively? (Pp. 718–724.)   ———

10. Does he use appraisals as a means of helping his subordinates to improve their performance? (Pp. 487–488.)   ———

11. Does he select, or recommend promotion of his subordinates, on the basis of his objective appraisal of their performance and in the light of the potential for growth in the company? (Pp. 484–501.)   ———

12. Does he take such steps and make such recommendations as he can to provide adequate and motivating compensation and conditions of work for his subordinates? (Pp. 454–456.)   ———

   Total number of questions on which ratings are made: ———
   Total score on questions given ratings: ———
   Average of ratings in STAFFING: ———

DIRECTING   RATING

1. Does he understand what motivates his subordinates and attempt to build into their position and position environment a situation to which these motivations will respond? (Pp. 566–588.)   ———

2. Does he so lead and guide his subordinates and interpret company and departmental objectives as to make them see that their own self-interest is in harmony with, although not necessarily the same as, the company's or department's goals? (Pp. 554–555.) _____

3. Does he issue instructions that are clear, within his authority, and fully understandable to his subordinates? (Pp. 557–560, 590–610.) _____

4. Does he use effective and efficient communications techniques in dealing with subordinates? (Pp. 590–610.) _____

5. Does he engage in an appropriate amount of face-to-face contact? (Pp. 250–251.) _____

6. Does he create an environment where people are encouraged to suggest innovation in product, process, marketing, or other company planning and policy areas? _____

7. Is he receptive to innovative ideas, suggestions, and the desire to be heard, whether from his superiors, his equals, or his subordinates? _____

8. Does he expect his subordinates to suggest changes or express objections to what they may regard as the wrong objectives, policies, and programs, or does he expect blind compliance with company policies and programs and his own decisions? _____

9. Can his subordinates reach him readily to discuss their problems and obtain guidance? _____

10. Does he help his subordinates to become oriented to the company's programs, objectives, and environment? _____

11. Does he exercise participative leadership when useful and authoritative direction when necessary? (Pp. 627–629.) _____

12. Is he effective as a leader ("the capacity and will to rally men and women to a common purpose")? (Pp. 612–619.) _____

Total number of questions on which ratings are made: _____
Total score on questions given ratings: _____
Average of ratings in DIRECTING: _____

CONTROLLING   RATING

1. How effectively does he tailor his control techniques and standards to reflect his plans? (Pp. 639–644.) _____

2. Does he use control techniques, where possible, to anticipate deviations from plans? (Pp. 644, 647–648.) _____

3. Do his control techniques and information promptly report deviations from plans? (P. 644.) _____

4. Does he develop and rely upon objective or verifiable control information? (P. 645.) _____

5. Does he develop controls that point up exceptions at critical points? (Pp. 644–645.) _____

6. Are his control techniques and information designed to show exactly where in the organization deviations occur? (P. 646.) _____

7. Are his control techniques and information understandable to those who must take action? (P. 647.) _____

8. Does he take prompt action when unplanned variations in performance occur? (Pp. 644, 647–648.) _____

9. When deviations from his subordinates' plans occur, does he help them take action? _____

10. Does he operate effectively under variable (budget) profit and performance plans? (Pp. 655–659.) _____

11. Does he supplement his (budget) profit and performance plans with other devices of control? (Pp. 659–662, 664–691.) _____

12. Does he recognize and implement the network nature of his planning and control problems? (Pp. 681–686.) _____

13. Does he keep abreast of, and utilize, newer techniques of planning and control? (Pp. 664–691.) _____

14. Does he develop and utilize overall methods of control of performance, where suitable, in his operations? (Pp. 694–712.) _____

15. Does he help his subordinates develop control techniques and information that will show *them* how well *they* are doing in order to assist in "control by self-control"? _____

16. Does he keep his superior informed of significant (to his superior) problems and errors in his operation, their causes, and steps being taken to correct them? _____

Total number of questions on which ratings are made: _____
Total score on questions given ratings: _____
Average of ratings in CONTROLLING: _____

SUMMARY:

Both the superior and the subordinate, no doubt, will be interested in the statistical data concerning the evaluation. In each area the average is calculated on the basis of questions answered.

No. of Questions	Principles	No. of "Not Known" or "Inapplicable"	No. Questions Answered	Total Count	Average Rating
14	Planning				
19	Organizing				
12	Staffing				
12	Directing				
16	Controlling				
73					
TOTAL:					

Evaluation of: _____

Completed by: _____

Date: _____

Forms for Summary Report of Appraisal of Managers as Managers

PERFORMANCE AS A MANAGER SUMMARY

NAME _____ POSITION _____ DIVISION/COMPANY _____

BASIC	SUMMARY SCORES		SUPERIOR'S COMMENTS	SUPERIOR'S SUPERIOR'S COMMENTS
	Previous Year	Current Year	Rated by _____ Date _____	By _____ Date _____
PLANNING				
ORGANIZING				
STAFFING				
DIRECTING				
CONTROLLING				
TOTAL AVERAGE				

SUMMARY RECOMMENDATIONS
TO MY SUPERIOR

Name:_____Title:_____Co./Div. _____

I. My Review of My Performance

   A. General Statement on my Performance as a Manager (Exhibit B)

   B. General Statement on Performance Against My Goals

Date:_____   Signed:_____

SUMMARY RECOMMENDATIONS
TO
REVIEW COMMITTEE

PARTICIPANT:_____ COMPANY/DIVISION:_____

I. REVIEW BY SUPERIOR
  A. **General Statement on Performance as a Manager**

  B. **General Statement on Performance Against Goals**

  C. **Recommendation for Bonus:**   _____% of Presumptive Bonus
     Because:

          Subordinate's annual salary   Superior's
                                                Signature:_____ _____
          as of Sept. 30_____   Date:_____

II. SUPERIOR'S SUPERIOR (comments on above)

Recommendation for Bonus: _____% of Presumptive Bonus

  Date:_____   Signed:_____

Examples of Summary Report
of Appraisal of a Manager
as a Manager

*(with Summary Recommendations
to Review Committee)*

Example I
PERFORMANCE AS A MANAGER SUMMARY

Division
International—Europe
Subsidiary

Superior
W. C. Rossmore, Vice-President
International Operations

Subordinate
A. B. Williams
General Manager
—Europe

CONFIDENTIAL

BASIC	SUMMARY SCORES			
	Previous Year End	Current Year		
		1st half	2d half	
I. Planning	2.9	3.5	3.1	
II. Organizing	2.8	3.4	3.2	
III. Staffing	2.8	3.6	3.3	
IV. Directing	2.8	3.7	3.6	
V. Controlling	2.5	3.3	3.0	
Total	13.8	17.5	16.2	
Average	2.8	3.5	3.3	

Superior: Of my 6 subordinates rated,
I rate this subordinate member 1.
Superior's superior: Of this subordinate's
subordinates, I rate *this* subordinate
1.

SUPERIOR'S COMMENTS (in detail)

I. *Planning*

The profit planning of this division, including short-term and long-term goals, is well thought out, well set out, and related in a most positive way to those of the company. If anything, some of the planning could be more imaginative. He assists his subordinates in establishing viable goals for their operations. ABW has created an excellent climate in his area and utilizes excellent planning techniques for his own planning and as a coach for his subordinates. He understands company policy and takes it into consideration in his planning decisions. ABW recognizes the salient issues and plans accordingly. His plans, when presented to me, show considered analysis of alternatives, along with their advantages and disadvantages. He is mindful of the short-term and long-term costs of his planning decisions.

SUPERIOR'S SUPERIOR'S COMMENTS

Analysis excellent.
I agree.

222

II. Organizing

I gave ABW excellent marks in this category. He retains proper responsibility when delegating authority to his subordinates. He formalizes in writing his authority delegations to subordinates in a clear and precise manner. He does not have a tendency to create excessive levels of organization. He gives his subordinates worthwhile tasks to perform, the authority to perform them, and refrains from interfering with their getting the job done. He has created an excellent climate for accomplishment in his area. He does *not* make committee decisions, although his staff meetings are well prepared, utilizing proper agenda and preparation.

| I agree but would slightly increase his rating from an average of 3.3 for the year to 3.6. |

III. Staffing

Since becoming General Manager, ABW has selected key individuals who have (in my opinion) potential to assume greater responsibility. He does not keep subordinates who have questionable ability in their jobs (e.g., he "cleaned out" the entire Technical Products Division). He is objective in his appraisal of his subordinates, especially on their ability to manage effectively. ABW has some candidates who could emerge as a replacement for ABW (e.g., Joseph Richardson, Marketing Manager; Peter White, Chief Accountant). He retains full responsibility for staffing his company, although he does use professional assistance from a management firm to screen potential candidates.

| The rating in this area is somewhat low. |

SUPERIOR'S COMMENTS (in detail)	SUPERIOR'S SUPERIOR'S COMMENTS
IV. *Directing* ABW directs his subordinates so that they understand what the targets are and makes sure that his subordinates keep their eyes on the targets as established by the corporation. He does not "lock arms" with his people. He is the best leader I have in my immediate subordinates. He is receptive to innovation no matter where it comes from. He is aware of and up to date on what is going on. Is easily accessible to his subordinates (which is new for his area). He *is* in charge. I have been most pleasantly surprised by ABW's ability. He is dedicated and hard working. He is completely loyal and has built a healthy climate in his organization. His people are encouraged to suggest innovations in products, policies, and marketing areas. He asks a lot of his subordinates, but is completely fair.	I agree.
V. *Controlling* I find that ABW needs coaching in control techniques and how to use them to anticipate deviations from plans. He has good accounting and production control and is on top of the marketing of all products through close contact with his Marketing Manager and Sales	I have seen some cases where control was poorer than indicated here but rating in

Managers. He has the benefit of knowing the product operation from the ground up, having been associated with distributors, competitors, etc., for many years. His division has performed very effectively under variable budgeting. In general his control techniques point up where deviations in his organization occur, and he takes action! ABW keeps me completely informed of any significant problems, errors, or deviations in his operation along with recommended courses of action —no surprises.

total is approximately correct.

SUMMARY RECOMMENDATIONS TO REVIEW COMMITTEE

Participant: <u>A. B. Williams</u>   *Company/Division:* <u>General Manager—Europe</u>

I. Review by Superior

   A. *General Statement on Performance as a Manager*

   I have been most pleasantly surprised and pleased at the excellent manner in which ABW has taken over the responsibility as General Manager of Europe. At this point in time I would unhesitatingly say that he is the best International General Manager that we have. He is thoroughly knowledgeable about our company's goals, procedures, policies, and ambitions. He makes sure that the job gets done. His subordinates respond to his suggestions and requests. ABW runs a tight ship. I feel that we can build on him and consequently will help him during 1970 to strengthen his first-line managers so that he is echeloned should other opportunities become available which ABW would fit.

   B. *General Statement on Performance against Goals*

   ABW's performance against goals was the best of any General Manager's, and he consistently reported against goals concisely and on time, without a doubt the best performance of any General Manager in international operations. His sales and profits were 8 percent above goals. His share of market increased. His new product performance was 86 percent of sales goals and 95 percent of gross profit goals, despite failure in one product area, which he has now reorganized and in which he replaced the manager. His marketing program goals were met except for one promotion. He met inventory reduction goal and completed plans for a new facility in Germany.

   C. *Recommendation for Bonus:*   <u>130%</u> of Presumptive Bonus
   Because:

   ABW did an outstanding job as General Manager in his first year. He did an outstanding job while Acting General Manager, and when he became General Manager took hold of the reins and has piloted Europe to a record year in face of severe economic situations.

	Superior's
Subordinate's annual salary	Signature: <u>W. C. Rossmore</u>
as of Dec. 31 $30,000	Date: <u>2-12-70</u>

II. Superior's Superior (comments on above)

   I agree with above. I was lukewarm on ABW. It was my mistake that he was "Acting" GM for so long. Rossmore did an all-out job of looking for an outside GM but finally decided to promote ABW. ABW has surprised me in many positive ways.

   Recommendation for Bonus: <u>130%</u> of Presumptive Bonus
   Date: <u>2/20/70</u>   Signed: <u>H. C. Harvey</u>
                                                 President

Example II

PERFORMANCE AS A MANAGER SUMMARY

Participant: Frank E. Burke, Sales Manager

Superior: L. E. Jameson, Division Manager

Division: Building Products   *Superior's Superior:* H. C. Harvey, President

BASIC	SUMMARY SCORES		SUPERIOR'S COMMENTS	SUPERIOR'S SUPERIOR'S COMMENTS
	Previous Year	Current Year		
I. *Planning*	2.4	2.7		
II. *Organizing*	2.4	2.9		
III. *Staffing*	3.0	3.0		
IV. *Directing*	2.6	2.7		
V. *Controlling*	2.6	2.7		
Total average:	2.6	2.8		

SUPERIOR'S COMMENTS

I. *Planning*

Frank Burke approaches the planning function without undue force or pressure from his superior. Until recently he has tended to limit the participating of *all* who could be involved. We have discussed the matter and Frank promptly organized a Marketing Committee to provide such involvement. He is goal oriented and his plans are precise.

On the negative side, he sometimes fails to consider all available alternatives before making recommendations. This, I believe, will be improved by the increased input of a Marketing Committee. He needs to enlarge the scope and vision of his plans.

II. *Organizing*

In this respect Frank has shown much improvement because he himself is better organized. He requires his subordinates to organize their own efforts in fine fashion and helps them by providing necessary detailed data and objectives.

SUPERIOR'S SUPERIOR'S COMMENTS

Frank has an accounting background, and it is not peculiar that he lacks imagination in planning but is very thorough in detail. Fortunately he has an Assistant Manager who has an abundance of imagination. They do make a good team and the Marketing Committee influence should improve Frank's planning.

I have noted evidence in a number of areas that Frank has his department well organized.

	HSL – 2/17/70
III. *Staffing* In this regard I find little to criticize. His department is staffed with good people who know their jobs well. In Bill Jones, he has an excellent second-in-command. There is no deadwood or unnecessary layers of supervision in his department.	Agree with LEJ's comments.
IV. *Directing* His instructions are normally clear and precise. His people know what is expected of them and appear to respond well to his direction. Frank is not a "natural born leader" in terms of the normal interpretation, but his subordinates respect him and the position he holds. He plans to join Toastmasters to improve his personal effectiveness.	Agree with LEJ's comments. He needs to improve his impact on others in oral communication.
V. *Controlling* Frank's planning is goal oriented, and because his reports are related to those goals, he is promptly aware of deviations from the plan. He can improve as a manager, however, in terms of interpreting those deviations and taking appropriate advance steps to correct problems. His control of period expenses is excellent.	Agree with LEJ's comments.

SUMMARY RECOMMENDATIONS TO REVIEW COMMITTEE

Participant: Frank E. Burke, Sales Manager

Company/Division: Building Products Division

I. Review by Superior

    A. *General Statement on Performance as a Manager*

       Frank Burke is profit oriented (somewhat unusual for a sales mana-
ger) and reasonably well organized. He has improved considerably
in understanding the need for thorough preparation in his work
and implements that understanding. He has also shown improvement in his willingness and ability to enlist help from others. He
lacks imagination (therefore *needs* the help of others) and is not
a "born" leader of men.

    B. *General Statement on Performance against Goals*

       As related to formal goals, my estimate is 25 percent accomplished.
I am particularly critical of his goal covering a program for recap-
turing the Southern California market because in spite of available
volume a *program* could and should have been developed. This is
now being done but way behind schedule. However, his short-term
goals relative to "market" sales volume, special promotions, etc.,
have been well organized, measurable, and, in most instances, met.

    C. *Recommendation for Bonus:* 80% of Presumptive Bonus

       Because: The sales department for which he is responsible has made
a major contribution to profits, despite his missing or being late
on so many goals.

	Superior's
Subordinate's annual salary	Signature: L. E. Jameson
as of Dec. 28 $26,000.00	Date: 2/16/70

II. Superior's Superior (comments on above)

    Frank is not a strong leader. He lacks the imagination and leadership
one expects in a sales manager. Fortunately, he has an imaginative
assistant, which tends to make a good team in charge of the department.

    Overall performance—average.

Recommendation for Bonus:	90% of Presumptive Bonus
Date: 2/20/70	Signed: H. C. Harvey, President

Examples of Bonus Committee Summary Reviews and Awards

BONUS

	Presumed	$10,525.00
Bonus Committee	Bonus Committee	$13,700.00
Summary Review	PERCENTAGE RECOMMENDATIONS	
	Superior	160%
	Bonus Committee	130%

W. C. Rossmore, VP—International Operations

STRENGTHS

1. Sales and profit goals of international divisions exceeded.
2. New-product goal performance good, but missed slightly.
3. Exceptional improvement as a manager.
   a. Analyses of international General Managers outstanding.
   b. Analysis against goals (except Australia) good.
   c. Shows great strength and imagination in managerial areas.
   d. Good performance in personnel policy and direction good.

WEAKNESSES:

1. Did not achieve certain goals.
   a. Slightly missed new product goals.
   b. Slightly missed profit percentage goals.
   c. Inventory levels.
   d. Accounts receivable.
   e. Cash flow.
   f. Marketing sales promotion.
2. Failure to see that adequate goals were set and reset in Australia despite reorganization and plant move.
3. Has not built adequate international acquaintances in distribution.
4. Some deficiencies as a manager.
   a. Not been as successful as desirable in checking on subordinates' plans.
   b. Needs improvement in control techniques.
5. Inability to work well with German general manager and marketing manager.

	BONUS	
	Presumed	$5,720.00
	Bonus Committee	$4,600.00
Bonus Committee	PERCENTAGE RECOMMENDATIONS	
Summary Review	Superior	80%
	Superior's Superior	90%
	Bonus Committee	80%

Frank E. Burke, Sales Manager
Building Products Division

STRENGTHS:

1. Profit oriented.
2. Sales department has made major contributions to company sales growth and profits.
3. Short-term goals met.
4. Performance as a manager barely average.
   a. Has shown improvement in understanding need for preparation and to enlist help.
   b. Fairly thorough in planning.
   c. Good in organizing.
   d. Excellent in staffing—has good No. 2 man.
   e. Controls generally good but need improvement.

WEAKNESSES:

1. Lacks imagination.
2. Not too effective as a leader.
3. Performance as a manager needs improvement, particularly in directing where record is poor.
4. Missed many formal goals largely through late planning and implementation.

Bonus Committee
Summary Review

BONUS	
Presumed	$6,230.00
Bonus Committee	$5,600.00
PERCENTAGE RECOMMENDATIONS	
Superior	100%
Superior's Superior	95%
Bonus Committee	90%

S. E. Clark, Operations Manager
Chemical Division

STRENGTHS:

1. Loyal, dedicated, hardworking.
2. Met many significant goals.
   a. Savings in drum, etc., purchases.
   b. Freight savings.
   c. Savings in packaging labor.
   d. Inventory requisitioning system.
3. Has shown an improvement in managing—rated as "good."
   a. Good in directing.

WEAKNESSES:

1. In a division that has not contributed significantly to company profits.
2. Missed a number of goals.
   a. Quantitative goals 4, 5.
   b. Qualitative goals 2, 3, 4, 5.
3. Has a number of weaknesses in managing (perhaps a rating of 2.95 is too high).
   a. Has individual goals but does not filter these down through the ranks.
   b. Has not required enough of his people in setting and meeting their goals.
   c. Does not exact enough responsibility from subordinates.
   d. Inclined to do it himself rather than delegate.
   e. Inadequate in staffing.
   f. Needs better controls.

Index